Portrait of a Dancer, Memories of Balanchine
An Autobiography

Alice Patelson

VANTAGE PRESS
New York

To my parents,
Patricia and Henry,
and my sister, Sally,
with love

FIRST EDITION

Published by Vantage Press, Inc.
516 West 34th Street, New York, New York 10001

Manufactured in the United States of America
ISBN: 0-533-11378-4

Library of Congress Catalog Card No.: 94-90832

0 9 8 7 6 5 4 3 2 1

Contents

A Note to the Reader

The universal use of French to describe the steps and movements of ballet gives all dancers an international language. I have included a glossary of terms at the back of the book for clarification. The definitions are simplified descriptions of what the movements would look like when executed. The glossary also gives the reader an idea of the wide range and variety of exercises, steps, and movements. Since ballet is a visual and physical art form, it has always been taught from generation to generation by demonstration.

Chapter 1
Childhood

My mother was a dancer. She danced in Paris in 1937 with the Radio City Rockettes when they won first prize at the Exposition Internationale de Paris. She danced on Broadway and in Hollywood when MGM made all those great musicals in the 1940s. She danced with a USO show, entertaining the troops, during World War II and returned from Europe in 1946 when she met my father, just discharged from the army. A year later they were married. Dad rejoined his brother at the Joseph Patelson Music House on West Fifty-sixth Street behind Carnegie Hall. The Music House became a unique institution, serving musicians, composers, conductors, orchestras, singers, and opera houses all over the country. Down the street was the stage door of the City Center of Music and Drama, home of the New York City Ballet. George Balanchine was a customer.

I was born in New York City in Doctors Hospital. When I was two weeks old, Mom and Dad, my sister, Sally, our springer spaniel, Lady, and I moved to Merrick, Long Island, on the south shore. The year was 1952. Our home was a bungalow on a half-acre. It was a beautiful property in an old section with huge trees, perennial flowers, a grape arbor, and a small hut by an outside pump, which became a playhouse for us. It was hedged in and private, with just one house on the street.

1

Dad almost immediately started redesigning the bungalow. The walls were knocked down in order to create a large dining and living area, including a fireplace. An open staircase was built, which led to our bedrooms above. Not long after that was done, he put up ballet barres along the wall of the dining room. I guess I can say my dancing career began before I could walk.

One of my earliest memories is of my mother teaching students, while I wandered about the house. Before she started teaching, she attended a series of seminars given by Thalia Mara and Arthur Mahoney at Ballet Repertory on West Fifty-fourth Street. The seminars were designed to aid in teaching elementary ballet in properly graded levels of technique.

By the time I was five years old, our house was expanded to include a studio constructed off the dining room. Once again a wall, this time an outside wall, was knocked down, and a large studio was added, with a partition separating the dancing room from the dining area. One could observe the students without being seen, and I spent many hours watching my mother teaching basic ballet technique to the neighborhood children. My sister, Sally, was part of this group.

Before class, when my mother came downstairs dressed in her leotard, tights, and slippers, Lady knew it was time to go upstairs. Then, when she thought she couldn't be seen, she would run and make a flying leap, landing in the center of my parents' bed. When class was over, Mother would go up the steps, making sure that Lady could hear her, giving her plenty of time to get off the forbidden bed.

When I was six years old, my mother started a preballet class for me and others my age. We moved to music without the discipline of formal exercises. Mother was wonderful at choreographing a variety of numbers, which often required the use of props. I remember holding a paper umbrella as I daringly walked an imaginary tightrope to the music of Tchaikovsky. We also learned simple steps, such as *chassé* and polka. By the time I was eight, I began my first year of serious training. At this stage of development, a child is able to understand some of the basic concepts of ballet technique. We learned the five positions of the feet and did a series of exercises while holding onto the barre with one hand. My mother demonstrated and we imitated her. We started with the *pliés*. This was followed by *battements tendus, battements dégagés, ronds de jambe à terre, port de bras, battements frappés, petits battements sur le cou de pied, retirés, grands battements*, and *relevés*. The purpose of these exercises was to develop the muscles while developing the turnout. The legs and feet were turned out from the hips down. Turnout was never forced but was acquired gradually throughout the training. Each exercise at the barre had a specific function and prepared the body to execute the steps and movements. In the center we learned the five positions of the arms and repeated some of the exercises done at the barre. We practiced steps such as *glissade* and *balancé* and finished the lesson with a series of small jumps from first position, *temps levé*. Each jump began with a *demi-plié*. We would push off from the floor and spring into the air, stretching our legs and pointing our toes, landing again in the *demi-plié*, toes first, then bringing our heels down. We also practiced *changement* and *échappé*. We learned the French names of the exercises and steps as we did them.

Every year I looked forward to the annual open house. On these occasions the partition that separated the dancing room from the dining room was opened, and parents were invited to observe the class. Several rows of chairs were placed in the dining room, making a seating area for the audience. At the end of the lesson a curtain was drawn and we put on our tutus. My mother, with the help of my grandmother, made tutus that could be tied with pink satin ribbon around the waist over our leotards. There were short pink tutus for the younger students and longer white tutus with flowers for the older students. When the curtain was opened, we were a vision of accomplished ballerinas. We performed the ballets my mother had choreographed for an enthusiastic audience. My performances were not limited to these events only. Sally and I put on shows for my parents. I loved to choreograph and create my own ballets. Not only did we dance; we sang along with the records from *Oklahoma, Carousel, Brigadoon*, and *My Fair Lady*. My favorite role was Eliza Doolittle with her cockney accent, and like Eliza I was transformed into the heroine of my dreams.

I was never pressured to dance. I simply enjoyed exercising, but ballet was not my only interest. My parents had acquired a used baby grand piano, and I began taking lessons from a neighborhood teacher. Although ballet and music consumed most of my time, I loved to play on our property and spent a lot of time bike riding and throwing a basketball into a basket that was attached to our garage. There was a dirt driveway that ran across the yard at one end and was eventually paved because there were so many cars coming and going when mothers dropped off and picked up their children for classes. When classes were not in session, I used the driveway to roller-skate. In the summer we played badminton and baseball. Dad set up an aboveground swimming pool. It was round, four feet high, and twenty-four feet in diameter. We all loved to swim, including the neighborhood kids. One time we saw about fifteen blue jays lined up on the rim of the pool chattering away. One of the birds had fallen in, and Dad came to the rescue. Lady had free rein and always joined us when we were playing outside, especially at our cookouts, when we barbecued hot dogs and hamburgers and toasted marsh-mallows.

Camp Avenue Elementary School was within walking distance from our home. Sally started there and I followed in her footsteps. When I was in the third grade we were given an unusual test to judge our musical ability. The test was somewhat confusing, but I must have passed because I was the only one invited to go downstairs to the music room and choose an instrument, which I would be taught to play. Some of these instruments seemed quite formida-ble-looking to me, but I was drawn to the violin. The idea was that I would receive training for a year and then be able to join the school orchestra as well as continuing with the training. I had no illusion of being a great violinist. As a matter of fact, it became clear to me that I had more nat-ural ability on the piano than I did with the violin, but be-cause of my love of music I was a willing participant.

By the time I was nine years old, I started going into the city with Sally on Saturdays to study at Ballet Reperto-ry. She was four and a half years older than I was and took a more advanced class than I did. I had to wait a couple of hours until my turn came, and I used the time to watch Thalia Mara and her husband, Arthur Mahoney, alternate in giving a series of classes to a large group of students who were more advanced than the students who attended my mother's school. I was absolutely fascinated as I sat there and observed, and I believe that I made the decision then and there to become a dancer. As ballet became a driving interest for me, Sally simultaneously lost interest; by the time she was fifteen she quit dancing. Because of the difference in our ages, there was never any real competition between us.

We often went to see performances of the New York City Ballet at City Center. I was thrilled by Jacques D'Amboise soaring gracefully into the air in *Stars and Stripes* and inspired by Melissa Hayden and Allegra Kent. After one performance my father took us backstage. He introduced us to Balanchine, who was courtly and gracious. Not long afterward, when Balanchine was in the store, Dad mentioned to him that his daughters were studying ballet. Balanchine's response was: "Too many girls; make boys."

The Music House on Fifty-sixth Street had formerly been a carriage house, built in 1879. It had two stories. After my father's brother bought the building, it was completely renovated. A grand staircase was built leading up from the store to the second level, which had been divided into an office and an apartment for my uncle's family. I have vivid memories when we visited them of my cousin Danny, Sally, and me romping around the store and office, playing with the telephones and adding machines and riding the ladder downstairs in the aisle where the music was stored. When the employees came in the morning, it was evident that the Patelson kids had been there the night before. There was a statue of Beethoven in the entry hall, but we never disturbed that.

The Russian Tea Room on West Fifty-seventh Street was our favorite restaurant. We dined there on special occasions, and I remember stuffing myself on the delicious borscht and beef Stroganoff. In those days you could get a complete dinner for $7.95. Dad knew the maître d', who always tried to give us a large booth. The decor was unusual, with ornaments that hung from the ceiling, making it look like Christmas all year round. Before the restaurant became so widely popular, it was a hangout for musicians and dancers, and Balanchine was a patron.

We often came into the city to go to the Metropolitan Museum of Art or the Museum of Natural History with the sky show at the Hayden Planetarium. We bought Cracker

Jacks and fed the pigeons in Central Park and went to the zoo to watch the seals being fed. They were always performing, and being a performer myself, I related to them. At Christmastime we went to Rockefeller Center to see the tree and skaters and take in the show at Radio City. There was always a long line around the block, but we never had to stand on it because Mother was a member of the Rockette Alumnae and we could get our tickets at the box office without waiting. Sally and I felt rather important marching past all the other people.

Sometimes Mom, Sal, and I would come into the city to see a movie and then meet my dad after work. One time we invited Danny to come along to see *West Side Story*, with music by Bernstein and choreography by Jerome Robbins. It had been made into a film from the Broadway stage production. The impact of this film was so powerful and the violence so disturbing that I spent most of the time with my head in my mother's lap, avoiding the screen. The dancing was phenomenal. At that time Jerome Robbins was just a name on the screen to me. In 1969 he was very real when he returned to the New York City Ballet as a co-ballet master. I didn't realize then that as a member of the company I would be working with him. Most of the scenes from this film were shot on location on the West Side, where a slum area existed. A year or two later everything was torn down in order to make way for the Lincoln Center complex.

In 1961 my father suffered a massive heart attack. My parents had gone out to dinner and the theater, where he suddenly collapsed in the lobby. The manager was quick at getting an ambulance and rushing him to a local downtown hospital. My father's doctor, who lived in the city at the time, rushed to the scene and suggested that my dad be moved to New York Hospital, with which he was associated. Sally and I were at home with my grandmother. I did not fully understand what had happened, but for the first time I felt anxious and depressed. My mother took us to the hospital to visit, but I was not allowed to see Dad because I was too young. Frustrated, but not defeated, I wrote letters to my father. Fortunately for all of us, he recovered, though gradually, and just before Christmas my uncle brought him home from the hospital. I'll never forget how happy I felt when I saw him for the first time after six weeks. Lady in her excitement promptly peed on the kitchen floor and ran wildly about the house.

Not long after my father came home, a black cat marked with white paws came upon the scene. We could see her stalking birds in our yard, which we were not happy about, and making a nuisance of herself when we were out with Lady. Lady would scramble from window to window on different sides of the house looking out in frustration as the cat would casually wander by looking up at her. One day we heard a scratching at the door. When Dad opened it, with nosy Lady expectantly at his side, in walked the cat. Dad stared down at her, and Lady, with her feet braced wide, mouth open, eyes bugged out in shock, stepped back and let her pass. The cat, ignoring Lady and the rest of us, calmly inspected the studio and all the rooms downstairs while we watched in amazement. Then she went up the stairs to the bedrooms, with Lady bounding up after her and all of us following. When her inspection was over, she went down to the door, and when Dad opened it, she left.

We were bowled over. Lady was at the windows again, looking out frantically. Not long afterward the scratching was repeated. When the door opened, there she was again, this time with a kitten in her mouth. The same procession was repeated up the stairs to Sally's bedroom closet, where the cat laid the kitten down. This was repeated until there were three, and as Mittens licked them clean, Lady watched in fascination. It wasn't long before Lady was licking them and Mittens watched. She was now a member of the family.

My Grandmother Eine, who was my mother's mother, came to live with us when my grandfather died. She had been born and raised in Finland and had immigrated to this country in 1912. The Finns had a club for many years on the Upper East Side of Manhattan, where she performed, singing in a beautiful lyric soprano voice. I asked Grandma Eine to teach me to speak Finnish, and every night before bedtime I studied with her. We worked with a book called the *Aapinen*, which included poems and stories. I decided to memorize a poem and present it in school for our show-and-tell. I was not nervous as I stood in front of the class because I was used to being in front of an audience, but I was disappointed with their reaction. They seemed completely bewildered. I can't remember whether I translated or not, but at least the teacher appreciated my effort. Fortunately, I did not let this incident dampen my enthusiasm to learn more.

Grandma Elizabeth, who was my father's mother, often came to visit us. She had immigrated to this country from Romania in 1888 when she was a little girl. My grandfather came from Russia, but he died when my father was in high school, so I never knew him. Unlike Grandma Eine, who was very cheerful, Grandma Lizzie was somewhat depressed, and I thought it was my job to cheer her up. We often played cards. She taught me to play cassino and usually won the game. She did not like exercise and was not enthusiastic about ballet, but she did love music and encouraged me to play the piano.

Although I had made up my mind to be a dancer, I

spent a good deal of my time playing the piano. My technique and facility improved, and by the time I was ten I was playing early sonatas by Haydn, Mozart, and Beethoven. Dad brought home a tape recorder. It was a huge machine with two large taping reels. Sally and I spent hours talking into the machine, and one time, when I was playing the piano, she set up the microphone and made a recording. I no longer have it; I'm afraid this is lost to posterity.

When my mother taught, she used a record player in the studio. One day the students had arrived and just as we were going to begin class the machine broke. I raced from the dancing room to the living room, where I saved the day by playing some pieces from the *John Thompson Second Grade Book for Piano*. Mom was very pleased. I was kind of pleased, too, but I was a little sorry that I had missed class.

I did some composing after a while and showed it to my teacher. It was a sonatina and he said it was very good. In retrospect I don't think he thought I was a young Mozart, but I made a recording of it and this one I kept.

I had more confidence in myself as a dancer than as a pianist, but every year I mustered up the courage to participate in my teacher's annual recital. One year I was in the middle of playing the second-movement adagio from a Mozart sonata when I lost concentration. Even though the music was in front of me, I had lost my place. My teacher sat nearby to turn the pages. When I looked at him for help, his eyes were closed. I thought he was sleeping, but suddenly he opened his eyes just in time to put his finger on the exact place in the music where I had stopped. I finished the sonata. I'm not sure whether the audience was sleeping, but I finished the sonata.

By 1964 I had spent almost three years with Ballet Repertory. One day after class Thalia Mara approached me to ask whether I would like to join the academy. This consisted of academic courses coordinated with an intensive program of ballet. My parents and I decided that this was not the direction to go because I would not be able to receive an accredited high-school diploma. Also, even though Thalia and Arthur were good teachers, they did not have a ballet company. Instead, we decided that I would audition at the School of American Ballet, the official school of the New York City Ballet, under the direction of George Balanchine and Lincoln Kirstein. It was necessary to audition because the school only accepted children they thought had the potential to become ballet dancers.

On the day of the audition, my mother and I took the IRT subway from Penn Station up to Broadway and Seventy-ninth Street. Then we walked three blocks to Eighty-second Street, where the studios were located. Originally the school had opened in 1934 on Madison Avenue, but it had moved to this location in the 1950s. We climbed the long flight of stairs, and at the top of the steps was a large door with the name of the school. Inside was a long corridor with benches and a reception desk. I was shown to the dressing room, where I changed into my leotard, tights, and ballet slippers, after which I was taken to studio 3, a modest-sized room with an upright piano. There were three other girls auditioning along with me.

Soon afterward, a tall, dark-haired woman with a friendly manner came into the room. I recognized her to be Diana Adams, a former principal dancer with the company. Balanchine created *Agon* for her and Arthur Mitchell in 1957. She was accompanied by a shorter, older woman, Madame Tumkovsky, a teacher at the school. We took our places at the barre and began the first exercise, the traditional *plié*. Madame Tumkovsky was somewhat intimidating with her thick Russian accent and stern manner. She indicated what she wanted us to do, and I did it to the best of my ability. When I raised my leg in *grand battement*, she held it to examine the muscles. Finally, we moved away from the barre and stood in the center of the room, where we did some simple movements. Suddenly, Madame Tumkovsky said, "Make me *assemblé*."

Everyone stood as if frozen in their tracks. My training held me in good stead as I confidently executed four *assemblés*, moving forward. I was rewarded with a big approving smile on Madame Tumkovsky's face. During the audition I noticed that Diana Adams wrote in a notebook while she observed us. When it was over, I went into the hall to wait with my mother. After a while Diana came out and told us that I had been accepted at the school. It was evident that the others had not. Mother and I returned home to Long Island elated with my success. I felt that this was a turning point in my life.

Chapter 2
School of American Ballet

Since my mother had to teach her own classes, it was decided that my grandmother would accompany me to SAB for my lessons, which were to be on Mondays, Wednesdays, and Fridays at five o'clock. On the following Monday I found myself in studio 3 again with about twenty other girls who were approximately my age. I was eleven years old. I felt slightly uncomfortable as I took a place at the barre, because no one spoke a word to me. Everyone stared. I was a newcomer arriving in April, whereas they had been studying since September. Studio 3 had large windows facing Eighty-third Street and Broadway. Since we were on the second floor, we could see the passersby and they could see us as we stood at the barre.

A woman with a very good figure wearing a pair of black tights, black leotard and slippers, a turtleneck shirt, and a black leather belt entered the room and said, "Hello, girls." She was Elise Reiman, our teacher. Reiman had danced for Balanchine during the 1940s in Ballet Society, a company that preceded the establishment of the New York City Ballet.

Everyone turned their feet out in first position, and we began the *pliés*. We continued with the next exercise, which was *battement tendu*. Soon Reiman clapped her hands, stopping the music, and firmly reminded us that we were to point the foot in front of the nose. In my previous training, the *battement tendu devant* was done in line with the shoulder, but Balanchine wanted a crossed line and it was up to Reiman to instill this principle. We completed the rest of the barre work as Reiman demonstrated each exercise and we executed it. In the center we concentrated on *épaulement* (directions of the body). In this exercise, the head, arms, and legs were coordinated in various positions such as *croisé, éffacé,* and *écarté.* I had learned these positions thoroughly before coming to the school. At one point in the lesson, as we were traveling across the floor doing a combination of movements, once again, Reiman clapped her hands to stop the pianist and said, "Come on girls; let's have a little more energy." We finished the class with a series of small jumps, and at 6:30, after an hour and a half of strenuous exercise, we were dismissed. I was exhausted but happy with my first class. I realized that the competition was going to be fierce and that the atmosphere was a far cry from the protected environment of my mother's ballet school.

At the end of the term I asked the school if I could attend the summer session. Because of my age, they permitted me to take the ballet technique classes but not the point classes. I would have to wait until the fall term to go up on point. Because my class was scheduled at 9:30 in the morning, my mother and I got up at 6:30 A.M. in order to take the eight o'clock train to the city. I felt it was well worth the effort because Violette Verdy and Jillana, who were principal dancers with the company, taught regularly and I was inspired by their classes.

In the fall I made the switch from elementary school to my first year of junior high. The change is indelibly marked in my memory for several reasons. When I showed up for orchestra practice, I found myself to be located in the last

14

row of the second violin section. This was a humiliating demotion for me, since I had occupied the first chair of the first violin section at the Camp Avenue Elementary School. It seemed that the kids who had studied the violin privately had the edge over those of us who had studied at school. When the conductor said she was short of viola players, I eagerly volunteered to learn to play the viola. I felt it was a step up, since the four viola players would sit dead center behind the conductor and could be seen more easily by the audience. What I didn't realize was that it wasn't going to be easy to change my instrument. Every day I devoted fifteen minutes of my lunch hour, the only spare time I had, to go to the music room, where I interrupted the band rehearsal by having to get my viola out of a closet and my music out of a cabinet, after which I hastened to a soundproof room where I tried to master the instrument. My efforts were rewarded when we gave our spring concert and then made a recording. I still have it, and whenever I play it I keep listening to hear that viola.

My days at Brookside Junior High were hectic. I was permitted to leave an hour earlier than the other students in order to get to the city for my four o'clock class. I was in division A, which met three times a week plus an extra class on Saturday. I made a great mistake when I decided to travel with another ballet student who was in my class and lived on Long Island. We arranged to meet in the fifth car because she got on approximately twenty minutes into the ride after I did. It didn't take me long to discover that she was a very unpleasant girl. She criticized everything I said and wore. I was utterly miserable. I could hardly keep up with her as she ran from the Seventy-ninth Street subway station to the school. I would arrive just in time to hear her repeat everything I had said on the train to another student in the dressing room. I found a solution to my problem by telling her that I would be taking an earlier train, the 2:18. In order to meet this schedule I had exactly eighteen minutes for my mother to drive me from one end of town to the other. I made a mad dash as the bells were ringing and the gates were coming down. Thus I was initiated as an independent commuter.

There was an elegance about Muriel Stuart, who was one of my teachers that year. She had danced with Anna Pavlova's company during the 1920s and had been at the school since its inception. Our classes were held in studio 1, a very large room with a wooden floor, a high ceiling, a mirrored wall, and a grand piano. As one entered the studio, there was a platform, then a short flight of steps down. Off to the side of the studio was another room that led to the dressing rooms for the teachers.

We took our places at the barre and waited for Miss Stuart to come into the room. She was tall and slender and usually wore a long black silk skirt over her leotard. As soon as she arrived we started our *pliés*. One of the concepts that Stuart concentrated on was placement. We were taught to stand with the abdomen slightly pulled in and the diaphragm slightly lifted. The pelvis was centered and it was necessary to tighten the muscles of the thighs and buttocks. The neck, shoulders, and arms were supposed to be free of tension. We held our heads straight as we worked through the exercises. One hand rested lightly on the barre while the other arm was raised to the side slightly forward of the body. Some of these concepts were difficult to grasp at this stage of our development

In the center we practiced adagio, which was a combination of slow movements designed to develop balance. This consisted of *battement développé* in various directions while balancing on the supporting leg, as well as slow rotation on the supporting leg while the working leg was raised. Sometimes *pirouettes* were included with the adagio, but most often they were practiced as a separate exercise. I discovered early in my training that I liked to turn and had natural ability. We practiced *pirouettes en dehors* and *en dedans*. Usually the preparation for the *pirouette en dehors* was taken from fourth position (feet approximately one foot apart) bending both knees in *demi-plié*. One arm was held to the side, and the other was curved in front of the chest. Balanchine wanted it done with the front leg bent and the back leg straight, with one arm to the side and the other held straight in front of the chest with the palms of the hands facing downward. This was new for me, but I soon got used to it and preferred doing it that way. We did *tours chainés* and *tours piqués* traveling in a diagonal line across the floor. Correct timing of the head and arms was essential in mastering the turning movements.

We worked on jumping steps and combinations of movements. At first the arms were held low to the side. Then the head and arms were coordinated with the legs as we progressed. The idea was to make it look effortless, but this was hard to achieve. Some of the exercises done at the barre such as *battements frappés* and *petits battements sur le cou de pied* prepared us for jumps that required a beat. We did *entrechat quatre, royale,* and *entrechat trois*. The beats were made with the calves as the legs were stretched and the feet pointed, slightly opening the legs before and after each beat.

For the last fifteen minutes of the lesson, it was customary for us to sit down on the floor and change into our point shoes. Miss Stuart supervised us as we put lambs' wool on our toes and tied the pink satin ribbons across and around the ankle into a secure knot. We were taught to sew the ribbons on the shoe in exactly the right place to hold the shoe firmly without pulling over the instep. All toe shoes

17

were hand-made and varied considerably in quality and fitting. The shoes wore out very quickly, and a professional dancer could use one pair per performance. As students we wore the shoes many times before they wore out.

We stood up and faced the barre. With both hands holding on to the barre for support, we did *demi-plié* and *relevé* in first position. The foot was supported on as many toes as possible, not just the big toe. We practiced *soussus* from fifth position and *échappé* from fifth to second position, which required a slight spring onto the points. We were not permitted to practice in the center at that time because students had to take class every day before working extensively on point.

At the end of the year I received a letter from the school stating that I had been promoted into B, the intermediate division. I was relieved because I did not want to spend another year in A and felt that I was ready to move on. My family was making a trip to Europe, so I would not be attending the summer session. Sally had just graduated from high school, and I had turned thirteen. It would be the last opportunity that we would have to travel together, because soon we would all be going in new directions.

We flew by Pan Am to Rome. On the flight we met Hugo Fiorato, who was the associate conductor of the New York City Ballet. He was a frequent customer at the Music House and knew my father. The New York City Ballet was on tour in Europe at this time, and he was on his way over to meet them there.

From the airport a bus took us to the railroad station and deposited us to the sound and fury of Roman traffic. We were greeted on the street by a beautiful little boy with the face of a Renaissance angel. Dad said, "Massimo D'Azeglio." With great dispatch our bags were put in a cart, and with a grand gesture the boy led the way to our hotel.

It was a short walk and five lira away.

Rome was exciting and beautiful. We did the grand tour: the Coliseum, the Forum, Saint Peter's, the Vatican, Michelangelo's Sistine Chapel, the Borghese Gardens, the Trevi Fountain, and the Caracalla Baths, where we went for a performance of *Carmen*. To top it all, Sally and I got pinched by an irrepressible Italian.

We took the train to Florence, where we stayed in a charming but flea-ridden *pensione*, the Tornabuno Biacci. There was a lovely roof garden restaurant where we ate most of our meals. We walked through Florence, along the Arno River and over the Ponte Vecchio. We visited the palace art galleries, saw the sculptures, including the *David*, and traveled to the Michelangelo Piazza, overlooking the city. We made a trip to Fiesole, on the outskirts of Florence. There was a long view of the countryside and the ruins of an amphitheater.

Our next stop was Venice. When we came out of the train station we had a choice of a vaporetto or a gondola. Naturally we chose the gondola. The gondolier looked like a pirate with his hooked nose, swarthy complexion, and bandanna wrapped around his head. While Dad sang "O Sole Mio" the gondolier grinned as he poled our way down the canal to Pensione Academia.

Our next adventure was on our way to San Marco's Piazza. I stepped onto a crowded waterbus. It pulled away, leaving my family behind standing on the dock. My mother cried out and they must have understood what happened, because the boat came back and my family squeezed on. We visited San Marco's, the Bridge of Sighs, and the island where Saint Francis of Assisi is buried, and we swam and got sunburned at Lido Beach.

Dad said it was the Orient Express, but I'm not sure he got that right. It was the overnight train to Paris from

Venice. I did look out at the night sky and saw snow-covered mountains that must have been the Swiss Alps. In Paris we had reservations at the Hotel Cayré on the left bank, which was walking distance from the river Seine. We did a lot of walking in Paris: across the bridge to the Champs Élysées, the Arc de Triomphe, the Place de la Concorde, the Louvre, the Tuilleries, and the Paris Opera. Our excursions took us to the Sorbonne, the Pantheon, the Luxembourg Gardens, and Notre Dame. We certainly had to go up the Eiffel Tower to take in a view of the city. After a ride on the Bateau Mouche, we had to see the Grand Palace des Champs Élysées, where Mother danced with the Rockettes in 1937. We loved Paris. Who could not?

We flew to London and checked into our hotel, which was a disaster. The concierge was indifferent to our arrival and assigned rooms to us in an annex that was shabby, cold, and raw. We huddled before an electric heater built into the wall that radiated a minimum of heat. There were no other rooms available, and the food was terrible. To their surprise and indignation, we left the following morning. London was crowded, but we found rooms in the Hotel Piccadilly, near Trafalgar Square. These were fine and soon we were off to Big Ben, Parliament, 10 Downing Street, Westminster Abbey, the Tower of London, Harrods, Saint James Park and the changing of the guard at Buckingham Palace. We did not get to see the queen, but we felt welcome in London. We did have dinner with an old friend of my mother from her Hollywood days, Yolande Donlan, who was then a successful actress on stage and in films. She and her husband, Val Guest, who was a writer and film director, had a beautiful home in Saint John's Wood. I should say "half a home," as someone else had the other half. It once belonged to the mistress of George IV.

We engaged a graduate student of London University

to drive us out to Hampton Court, outside London. We found the palace and its beautiful gardens and got lost in a maze that was a fun game for the English court. After London, our same young Englishman, who was handsome and very pleasant, drove us to Oxford and Shakespeare country, where there were swans on the river Avon. We saw Blenheim and Warwick castles and drove through the Cotswolds, the beautiful English countryside. We stayed overnight at several charming inns. One evening at dinner Dad, who had a large acquaintance, heard a distinctive voice and, turning around, invited one of his Music House customers to join us. He and his wife were on a cycling tour through England. We visited Bath and Stonehenge and went on to Southampton, where we boarded the SS *France* to head home. It had been a fabulous trip, leaving us with memories that would last a lifetime.

In the fall I made the change from Brookside Junior High to the Professional Children's School on West Sixtieth Street off Broadway. The school arranged a schedule of academic studies to make it possible to get to a two-thirty class every day at the ballet school. There was no comparison between Brookside, the beautiful new school I left behind in Merrick, and PCS, a very old and unimpressive building. At Brookside the students moved from class to class, and at PCS in eighth grade we sat in one room while our teachers rotated. My classmates were Gelsey Kirkland, Colleen Neary, whose sister Pat Neary was a soloist with the company, and Elise Flagg. At two o'clock every day we raced down four flights of steps and ran a short block to Amsterdam Avenue, where we waited impatiently for the bus that took us uptown to Eighty-second Street. Then we ran another block to Broadway and up the flight of steps to SAB just in time to put on our ballet gear and start our *pliés*.

Felia Doubrovska was the ideal Balanchine dancer,

21

with her long legs and beautifully arched feet. In 1929 he created the role of the Siren for her in *Prodigal Son*. After retiring from performing, she was invited to teach at the school. I loved her classes and was able to improve my extension because she concentrated on giving a lot of adagio. We practiced large jumps such as *saut de basque* and *grand jeté*, and we worked on jumps with beats such as *brisé*. Sometimes Balanchine came in to watch. He would chat with Doubrovska in Russian. There was always a sense of excitement when he was in the studio. One day after class she said to me, "You can do everything. You can turn and jump and hold your leg up, but you have to point your feet more." I tried hard to improve my feet.

Doubrovska was married to Pierre Vladimiroff, who had been a premier danseur at the Maryinsky. I studied with him for two years before he retired from teaching. He loved the music of Chopin and often asked the pianist to play a waltz for some of the combinations we did in the center. There were three pianists who played regularly for our classes, but the school decided to try out a new pianist during one of Vladimiroff's lessons. When he requested a Chopin waltz the young man told him he was unable to play it. Then Vladimiroff said, "No music." We danced in silence, feeling slightly uncomfortable and very sorry for the young man. He did not get the job.

Toward the end of the lesson it was Vladimiroff's habit to cup his hands around his mouth and whisper, "*Fouetté*." This meant that he expected us to execute thirty-two *fouetté* turns. I always looked forward to this challenge. One time after I completed a combination of movements in the center, Vladimiroff followed me over to the barre, where I stood resting while another group of students worked on the combination. I was afraid he was going to criticize me, but instead he whispered in my ear, "You are not working; you are dancing."

During another class Vladimiroff was demonstrating when he suddenly lost his balance and fell flat on his back. We were stunned. His eyes were closed. Some of us rushed over to help him up. He refused any assistance and after a while he got up and finished the lesson.

Although I was no longer taking piano lessons because my schedule was so demanding, I continued to practice on my own. I was working on some of the Chopin nocturnes and waltzes and decided to surprise Vladimiroff by playing a piece for him. When he entered the studio I played a few bars from the waltz that is used in the finale of the ballet *Les Sylphides*. He stood and listened attentively, and I believe he was genuinely pleased.

In addition to my technique classes, I was taking two point classes a week with Stuart and Tumkovsky. The classes were an hour long and were difficult. We spent one half hour at the barre practicing exercises that strengthened the feet and ankles. In the center we did a variety of steps, including *pas de bourrée, passer,* and *bourrée*. As we gained strength we worked on turns. We mastered single *pirouettes* before attempting to do doubles. Stuart and Tumkovsky were completely different in their personalities and their approach. With Stuart we concentrated on muscular control and trying to look relaxed even though there was a great deal of tension in our bodies. With Tumkovsky strength was built through force and the repetition of exercises and combinations. I benefited from both teachers, but no matter who taught the class, at the end of the lesson my feet were sore.

On Saturday mornings we took a class in modern dance with Janet Collins. A large part of our time was spent sitting on the floor in bare feet doing various exercises and movements. It was not my favorite class. The best I can say for it was that at the end of the lesson I had a sore bottom instead of sore feet. I really preferred to be in my point shoes up on my toes and moving in a classical manner.

One evening in November I went into studio 3 to change into point shoes in preparation for my class. It was a little after five o'clock and already dark out. I sat on the floor, and a few minutes later the lights went out. I realized that the lights were not just out in the studio, because there were no streetlights on either. I left quickly and tried to find my way to the dressing room along with two other classes of younger students that had been in session. There was chaos in the dressing room, but I finally managed to find my locker and get dressed. My father usually met me at Penn Station, but I knew the subways would not be running and assumed that he would still be at the Music House. Two classmates joined me to walk down Broadway to Fifty-sixth Street. It was scary, but we arrived safe and sound. My friends continued on because the father of one of the girls had an office downtown. Dad and I stayed overnight, and we learned the next day that it had been an extensive blackout all over the eastern seaboard. So that's where I was when the lights went out.

Balanchine choreographed his production of the *Nutcracker* at City Center in 1954. When the company moved to the State Theater in Lincoln Center, the production became so popular that tickets were sold out well in advance. Every year students from the school auditioned, and when I was thirteen I went to the theater to try out for a part as a candy cane. Una Kai and Vicki Simon auditioned us. We had to perform a series of *jetés* traveling in a diagonal line across the rehearsal hall. After that Vicki demonstrated a combi-

prologue of *The Sleeping Beauty* provided excellent material for the students to work on. I developed endurance and a sense of style. Danilova demonstrated each variation, and two at a time we danced it for her. When a student danced well Danilova said in Russian, "Kha-ra-shoh (good)."

After I had been at the school for some time Balanchine decided that each division should wear a different color leotard. When I was in B we wore light blue. In C we wore white for variations and black for the other classes. Danilova always wore a bright-colored leotard with matching skirt and a scarf over her hair tied under her chin. Balanchine also decided that instead of wearing ballet slippers for the technique classes we were to wear soft point shoes. In other words, shoes that could no longer be worn for the variations, adagio, and point classes were to be worn for the technique classes. In the children's divisions ballet slippers were still worn.

The adagio class was taught by Andre Eglevsky, a former principal dancer with the New York City Ballet. In this class the boys were taught to partner the girls. For the first twenty minutes Eglevsky gave the girls exercises at the barre on point as a warm-up in preparation to dance. In the center he would demonstrate by partnering one of the girls, holding her waist or hand while she executed the combination. Then the boys asked the girls to dance. Unfortunately, there were more girls than boys and Eglevsky allowed the boys to decide with whom they would dance. The result was that tall boys were dancing with short girls and tall girls were dancing with short boys. Some of the girls were dancing a lot and some very little or not at all. During one class I was standing by the barre waiting hopefully for someone to approach me. A young man with a very nice manner came up to me and politely asked me to dance. The problem was that I was five feet, seven and a half inches tall and he appeared to be five feet, six inches tall. A little disappointed, but extremely grateful, I accepted his invitation. On point I towered over him by at least half a foot, but I was determined to dance. Not only did we do the exercises that were given, but we danced the pas de deux from *Swan Lake*, which Eglevsky was teaching us. This presented an even greater challenge because in this pas de deux the swan executed a series of finger turns. In order to do this I noticed my partner rising up on half-toe to reach my hand, which was overhead. He was just barely able to give me his finger to hold as I executed a *développé front*, carrying my leg to the side and then doing a series of turns. We would never have been cast onstage together, but we tried hard to create a romantic illusion.

The ballerina is dependent on her partner, but both must learn to time and coordinate their movements. The boy must put her properly on balance, and if he is lifting her, he must time the lift. If he lifts too soon, he creates a labored impression, and if he lifts too late, she looks ungainly. In the traveling lift, her partner must put her down on balance so that she can start the next step. If he is careless in setting her on point, her feet can be injured. When doing *pirouettes*, the girl turns within her partner's hands while one hand controls her speed and acts as a brake. He stops her after a certain number of turns, and the cavalier who stops her too soon, when she could have done one more, is in for trouble.

The boys took technique classes separately from the girls. The beginning training is much the same for the boys and girls. Because of the anatomical differences, the boys have different qualities and limitations. For example, boys' insteps are not as high as the girls' and they never dance on point. The strength in their feet is used for larger jumps, and they are able to do more *pirouettes*. The girl's balancing surface in a *pirouette* is limited to the blocked point of her toe shoe, whereas a boy has the whole ball of his foot. In general, a boy moves more slowly and jumps higher, covering more ground. Boys are expected to excel in *batterie* (jumps with beats). *Port de bras* should be flowing and graceful but masculine.

It was announced that Balanchine would be teaching one of our morning classes. There was a sense of excitement and trepidation as we anticipated the lesson. We took our places at the barre, and Balanchine entered the studio. He was sixty-three years old at that time but had a youthful appearance. We started the *pliés* and completed the rest of the barre work at a rapid pace, stopping occasionally when he gave a correction. In the center we practiced a variety of steps. I remember Balanchine standing in front of me and watching while I executed a double *pirouette* on point. Usually we did not work on point in the morning class, but we were expected to do so for this lesson. He had reminded us to keep the back leg straight for the preparation of the turn, and I felt that I had done it well.

Suzanne Farrell, a principal dancer with the company, taught one of our classes. Balanchine had choreographed the role of Dulcinea for her in *Don Quixote*. Advanced students were supers in this production. I played the part of a pig as we stampeded across the stage, and I walked in the funeral procession at the end of the ballet. It was somewhat hazardous because we wore long garments while descending a flight of steps from the wing to the stage. I was always afraid of tripping but didn't. I identified with Suzanne Farrell because we were the same height. She was twenty-two years old, and I was fifteen. When we were at the barre, she came over especially to watch me do *rond de jambe à terre*. In the center she stressed the energy she wanted to see in our movements.

Two years before I got into the advanced division, Balanchine asked Danilova to start a workshop, which meant that the students would learn either a complete ballet or selections from a ballet to be performed in the spring. This year she was working on *Paquita*, with lovely music by Minkus. Rehearsals were held in the evenings. There were parts for eight girls in the corps de ballet and several solo parts. I was devastated when she chose eight students to dance, leaving me and several others to be understudies. I could not understand why they were chosen and I was not. I never got to perform it, and during the spring I was out for almost a month with a bad case of tonsillitis. This was unusual for me because I was hardly ever ill. When I returned to the school, I was weak and thin but made plans to attend the summer session, still depressed over being left out of the workshop.

Many students from ballet schools all over the country came to study in the summer with the hope of being offered a scholarship. The studios were excruciatingly hot. We perspired profusely, and there was always an extra-long line at the water fountain. During one of my classes with Eglevsky I noticed that a man came in to observe. Afterward I was surprised when Eglevsky introduced me and another student to the director of the Ballets de San Juan. He was looking for students to work with his company during August. It was 1968, and I had just turned sixteen. I was thrilled to be chosen and given this opportunity. There were to be two weeks of rehearsals in Puerto Rico followed by performances in El Salvador, Costa Rica, and Guatemala. When I talked it over with my parents they were concerned about my being on my own as well as the instability in that region of the world. The problem was resolved when the other student's mother offered to accompany us on the entire trip. After my father talked to Eglevsky to learn more about the directors and the company, my parents decided to let me take the job.

My mother flew down with me for the two-week rehearsal period. Both mothers stayed at a hotel in the center of San Juan while we dancers stayed in a little house in front of the studio where we rehearsed. The house was a one-story structure with a wrought-iron gate for a front door. We soon discovered there was a variety of insects living with us because of the open door and windows without screens. Every night it became a ritual to spray the walls and moldings with Raid.

Ana Garcia and Juan Anduze were the directors of the company. Though it was a modest-sized company the level of its competence was comparatively professional. Earle Sieveling, who was a soloist with the New York City Ballet, was a guest artist. Class was held in the morning, followed by rehearsals for the rest of the day. I had to learn five ballets in two weeks. Most of the ballets were choreographed by Ana and Juan, but they also presented Balanchine's *Valse Fantasia*, with music by Glinka. I danced in Ana's *Nocturno*, which was classical in style, and Juan's *Los Comediantes, Petroglifos*, and *Urayoan. Los Comediantes* was humorous and *Petroglifos* was modern. *Urayoan* was a story ballet about the Spanish and Indians based on an event in Puerto Rican history. We did the second act of the *Nutcracker*, in which I danced "Waltz of the Flowers" and Juan choreographed "Marzipan" for me and the other student. Because we were under pressure to learn so much so quickly, I found it helpful to write down all of the choreography in a notebook every evening before I went to sleep.

After a grueling two weeks, my mother went home and we flew Taca Airlines to San Salvador. The audiences were small but appreciative, and some fans came to our dressing room afterward to ask for autographs. The condition of the dressing rooms was poor, and the stage was small, with hardly any wing space. We took class onstage using portable barres and rehearsed the ballets we were performing. Then we were given a break for dinner and came back to the theater to put on our makeup and warm up for the performance. Afterward there was another dinner served at the hotel for the whole company. We were warned not to drink the water.

El Salvador was a poor country. The people were shabbily dressed, the children barefoot on the streets, the buildings drab and rundown. In the center of the city was an open market where vegetables, fruit, and meats were sold under unsanitary conditions. In contrast, outside of the city there were wealthy homes on large estates. By comparison in San José, Costa Rica, the general appearance of the city and the people was one of more affluence and the theater and hotel were superior. One unforgettable experience was climbing up a volcanic mountain and looking down into the crater. We were supposed to continue on to Guatemala, but because of the political unrest and the murder of a U.S. diplomat, the tour was canceled.

For a young American girl like myself, observing the living conditions of the people of Central America, the poverty and differences in our culture, was an eye-opening experience. This tour was also excellent preparation for the New York City Ballet, where the ability to learn a ballet quickly and perform it on short notice was essential.

Chapter 4

Attaining the Goal

When I returned to the school in the fall I was dismayed when Diana Adams approached me to say that I should have asked permission from the school before taking a job. I told her that I didn't know and that Eglevsky had selected me. Apparently, there was a rule that students on scholarship had to ask permission, but when I was given a scholarship at the beginning of the intermediate division no one had informed me or my parents of the rules. I felt that Diana was more concerned about my breaking the rule than she was appreciative of what I had done and accomplished.

During the spring Stanley Williams started rehearsals for his workshop. He had danced with the Royal Danish Ballet and was teaching in Denmark when Balanchine invited him to join the faculty of SAB. His classes were very popular with company members, and a great many of them took my class regularly. During the three years I had studied with him he never gave me special attention and I was somewhat discouraged by his lack of interest. He had a tendency to correct company members and a few students whom he favored. For the workshop he was using selections from *Napoli* and had cast a group of short dancers for the parts. A few weeks after rehearsals had begun, my name was posted on the bulletin board along with those of another girl who was my height and a third girl who was shorter to learn a pas de trois. After one of his classes, he asked me and the other tall girl to stay and learn one of the sections. The third girl was to join us in two other dances. He demonstrated quickly a complex combination of *pas de bourrée* steps. Then he turned around to watch us do it. The other girl seemed to be in shock, but I was able to dance it for him. After this incident his attitude toward me changed. He called me by name in class and occasionally corrected me.

Around this time I started taking private lessons with Peter Nelson on Sundays. He had been recommended to my mother by another student's mother. Peter was a wonderful teacher. He had been a principal dancer with the San Francisco Ballet and also danced with the Ballet Russe de Monte Carlo. He had his own school and coached students who were moving toward professional careers as well as dancers with the New York City Ballet, Ballet Theater, and other companies. It was important to have special attention, not only for technical proficiency, but also for moral support. Classes were large at SAB, and because of the attitude of some of the teachers, with favoritism shown to some students and indifference to others, there was a highly competitive and sometimes depressing atmosphere. Although I had a tremendous will to dance, I found that having Peter's support made a real difference.

Danilova was doing *Les Sylphides* for the workshop and Frederick Franklin, who had danced with her in the Ballet Russe de Monte Carlo, came to our rehearsals to assist in teaching the choreography. This time all the students were given the opportunity to participate and Balanchine chose three members of the company to dance the leading roles. There was very little dancing for the corps de ballet. We danced in the opening section and the finale, and much of the time we posed in various positions while the soloist danced. Some of these positions were very awkward to sustain. For example, we had to get on the floor, where we lay with one leg extended and the other leg bent, leaning on one hand with the other hand posed in front of the chest, our backs slightly twisted and our heads turned away from center stage. Usually there was a pianist for the performance, but Balanchine wanted an orchestra and it was decided that the Teachers College Symphony Orchestra would be used. We all met uptown at the university to rehearse with the musicians. It was the first time I had ever rehearsed with Balanchine. The floor was so slippery that what had been relatively easy to do in the studio became an obstacle course here. Because the incentive to dance for Balanchine was so great, everyone danced full out, and, thankfully, no one fell down. The musicians turned out to be very good and the performances of both *Les Sylphides* and *Napoli* were given at the State Theater. A few days later Doubrovska told me that my feet had looked good.

At the end of the year two students from my class were selected to join the company. I was extremely upset and I believe the remaining students were as well. In addition to this disappointment, I received a letter from the school stating that I was not being promoted to D, the professional division. Instead I was expected to spend a third year in C.

In the fall SAB moved to the third floor of Juilliard in Lincoln Center on Sixty-sixth Street and Broadway. It was a beautiful school with spacious studios and dressing rooms. The schedule of classes was posted on the bulletin board, and I saw that Diana Adams was scheduled to teach one of my classes. It was unusual for her to be teaching. I was disturbed at the prospect of spending another year in C and felt they were not evaluating my work properly. To my great relief and happiness, after I took one class with her she promoted me to D. In this class, students were considered ready for professional work.

Sometime during October, I began to experience pain in my right foot. It became progressively worse and I was forced to let Diana know that I needed to rest the foot. It was the first time that I was injured in all the years that I had been dancing. Diana gave me a list of doctors, but I did not see anyone because I thought it would get better with rest and soaking. When I came back to the school my foot was still weak and painful, but I was able to take class with the hope that it would get stronger. At this time six girls from my class were selected to be apprentices with the company. I was heartbroken at missing this opportunity because I felt that if my foot had not been injured, I might have been chosen.

A couple of months later an audition for the Metropolitan Opera Ballet was posted on the bulletin board and all students in D were required to go. There was no guarantee that every student would get into the New York City Ballet, and when other companies needed dancers they notified SAB. The audition was held at the Metropolitan Opera House in Lincoln Center. I went with six or seven others from my class. The studio was crowded with dancers, and it seemed as if there were at least seventy-five people there. There was barely enough room to do the exercises at the barre, and we had to do the *grands battements* in two separate groups to avoid hitting each other. In the center they asked us to perform various combinations, including some Spanish-style movements. Then they asked the boys to partner the girls and we did some adagio. Finally the girls were required to do *fouettés* on point. The *fouetté* was a difficult turn to execute because it involved a series of turns on one leg whipping the other leg in a quarter-circle front to side while turning. I believe I was the only one left turning. Everyone else had given up. A few days later Diana told me that I was the only one in my class to be accepted by the Met. She also told me not to take the job. I was encouraged by what she had said because I interpreted it to mean that she was planning on putting me in the company.

Meanwhile Danilova was doing *Coppelia* for the workshop. She cast the tall girls to dance in one number and shorter girls and boys to dance in another section. There were two casts for the solo roles except for the Dawn variation. She allowed one dancer to dance the role in both casts. This dancer happened to have been accepted as an apprentice to the company earlier in the year but was rejected and returned to the school. I was cast with the tall girls but wanted very much to dance the Dawn variation because I felt it was suited to my abilities. I made a recording of the music on a small tape recorder that I brought to the studio and rehearsed the variation every day by myself until I was satisfied with the way that I did it. The variation began with some adagio movements that included promenade in *arabesque, développé écarté*, and balancing in *piqué arabesque*. The rest of the variation consisted of jumping steps, finishing with eight *saut de basques* in a circle, a large jump from one leg onto the other while turning in the air with one foot raised and pointed below the knee.

My parents encouraged me to speak to Diana Adams about dancing the variation for the workshop. I was nervous when I went into Diana's office to talk to her but managed to express the idea that I felt that the workshop should be an opportunity for all the students and that Danilova was permitting one girl to dance in both casts. I said that I would like to dance the role of the Dawn in the second cast. Diana's reaction to me was very positive, and she said she would speak to Madame Danilova. A few days later I was in the dressing room after class when Diana came in to tell me that she had spoken to Danilova and I was to dance the variation at the next rehearsal. She indicated that it was not definite that I would perform it, because that would be up to Danilova to decide. When the time came in rehearsal, to everyone's surprise, Danilova called my name to dance the variation. In a way I had challenged Danilova, and now I had to prove myself. I danced the variation and when it was over, to my amazement, everyone applauded. Danilova said, "Kha-ra-shoh," and from then on I danced it for the remaining rehearsals and the performance.

At this time I was also rehearsing another variation for my graduation ceremonies. As PCS was a special school for students who studied or worked in the performing arts, at graduation the seniors put on a show for the parents and faculty and each student had an opportunity to show off his or her expertise. I had chosen a variation from *La Bayadére*, and Danilova allowed me and another student who was graduating to rehearse during our variations class. In this variation one had to have an ability in turns, jumps, and extension (raising and holding the leg up).

A couple of weeks before we were to give the workshop performance I came into class one morning and after doing the *pliés* I felt an intense pain in my left knee. Something was terribly wrong, but I managed to get through the rest of the class. My knee was swollen and inflamed, but I decided not to tell anyone about the problem. I couldn't face missing the performance and made up my mind to go through with it. The performance was to be given at the State Theater. Parents and faculty were invited to watch, and usually Balanchine and Una Kai, the ballet mistress, came as well. On the day of the performance I went to the theater, where Stanley Williams gave a warm-up class in the practice room on the fifth floor. Then we went down to

38

the stage level, where we changed into our costumes. There were to be two performances, the first cast dancing in the afternoon and the second cast dancing in the evening. I danced with the tall girls in the first performance, and after doing my part, I remained in the wings to watch the other student dance the Dawn variation. At the dress rehearsal we had talked to the pianist about the tempo and he had agreed to play it fast for her and more slowly for me. I couldn't believe my ears. He was playing it slowly for her, thinking I was performing. The piano had been set up on a platform to the left of the stage, and he was unable to see the dancer. When the performance was over, I searched in vain for him. It was inevitable that I would have to perform it at whatever tempo he would play, and I knew it was going to be fast.

We did not have too much time to rest between the performances, and soon I was putting on the tutu for the Dawn variation. When I came out onstage the tempo was fast, as I had anticipated, but because the first movements were adagio it did not pose too much of a problem. When I got to the jumping steps, it seemed as if the tempo suddenly accelerated. I made a great effort to speed up my body and frantically whipped through the combinations of steps. Finally I took my preparation for the *saut de basques* in a circle and hurled myself through the air with lightening speed. When it was over the audience applauded, but I knew I had not danced it as well as I had in the rehearsal studio.

Graduation was held at the Juilliard Theater and I went ahead of time to put my makeup on and warm up for the performance. Madame Pourmel, who was wardrobe mistress for the company, had selected a white tutu for my variation. When it was my turn to dance, I was relieved because the tempo turned out to be perfect and I felt that I had danced well. It was customary for the school to have two well-known performing artists as guest speakers. This year they were Tammy Grimes and Edward Villella, a principal dancer with the New York City Ballet. After the show was over, we donned our caps and gowns and I was thrilled to receive my diploma from Edward Villella, a dancer I admired so much. Afterward at the reception Diana Adams, who had been watching, came over to congratulate me.

Balanchine was mounting a new production of *Firebird*, and Jerome Robbins was choreographing the monster section. They needed extra dancers for this section, and I was chosen along with three other girls to be apprentices. We were to rehearse and perform at the State Theater and do some additional performances in Saratoga, the company's summer home. I had no difficulty with my role as a monster. I can't say it was an auspicious beginning with the New York City Ballet, but it was a beginning. During July the four of us took a bus upstate. Since we had already started the summer course at the school, we were expected to return and finish the session when performances were over.

Saratoga is a small town noted for its health spas and racetrack. The theater was located on expansive grounds in the state park. The stage was outdoors, with a roof overhead.

Balanchine taught company class, which was held in a large air-conditioned studio, and I noticed that Una Kai came in to observe. She had her eye on the apprentices. One of the differences between Balanchine's class and classes at the school was that we did all of the exercises at the barre at a much faster tempo. When I wasn't rehearsing I sat in the audience watching Balanchine rehearse the company onstage, and when I wasn't performing I stood in the wings or went out front to observe. I learned a great deal by watching, just as I had so many years ago at Ballet Repertory. At the end of an exciting week, I returned to the school to finish the summer course.

We had August off and because my knee was still bothering me, it was a chance to rest. My parents rented a guest house on an estate in Connecticut, and I joined them for a week of relaxation. We had the use of a pool on the property. The owner invited guests up for the weekend, and one of the guests was a doctor. While I was at the pool he showed a real interest in me and I was flattered by his attention, but at the same time a little uncomfortable because he seemed so much older than myself. When I got back to New York, he called to ask me out to dinner at the Russian Tea Room. Although it was my favorite restaurant, I was a little leery of going out with an older man, so I asked Sally if she would come with me and the three of us went to the restaurant. I couldn't think of a thing to say, but Sally seemed to be handling it just fine and soon he was focusing on her and I could relax and enjoy my beef Stroganoff. I simply wasn't ready to concentrate on anything but my dancing.

I returned to SAB in the fall with high hopes of getting into the company. There was no guarantee that the apprentices would be accepted. I was taking class with Stanley Williams one morning in October when Una Kai came in to watch. I sensed that she was there to choose dancers for the company. Vicki Simon, who happened to be taking class, told me to move forward into the front line. I moved forward quickly so that Una could see me. Shortly afterward Balanchine came in. After class no one said anything to me, but while I was in the dressing room Suzanne Farrell, who had been taking class, came over and said, "Congratulations." Apparently a rumor had spread that I was in. Suzanne had left the company the year before and would

41

be joining the Béjart Company with her husband, Paul Mejia. Finally the secretary told me that Madame Molostwoff wanted to see me. Natalie Molostwoff was an administrative director and had been with the school since 1938. I went into her office, and she told me that Balanchine would like me to join the company. It was a great moment for me. It was almost seven years since I had come to the school with the goal of getting into the company, and now I had attained what I wanted. The year was 1970.

During my time at the school the level of technical ability had increased, and with the workshop added to the curriculum, the standard was higher and the competition greater than at any previous time. Compared to the number of students who studied at the school, relatively few were chosen to join the company. There were three qualities that were essential to have if one was to become a dancer: drive, dedication, and discipline, as well as a belief in oneself.

Chapter 5
George Balanchine and the New York City Ballet

The next day I made my way to the State Theater, where I was thrust into the dynamic pace of the New York City Ballet. Balanchine was teaching class in the main hall on the fifth floor. When I entered the studio there were already many dancers warming up at the barre. It was necessary to prepare for the lesson because of the fast tempo at which he worked. I took a place at the barre and began to do some *pliés*. The main hall was a huge room with no windows. Near the entrance was a bulletin board with the day's schedule of rehearsals posted. On the opposite side of the room was a grand piano, and at the farther end was a second entrance through which Balanchine arrived a few minutes late. He was sixty-six years old and looked a little older and heavier now, but there was an elegance about his movements.

We started the *pliés* to the tune of "Bali Ha'i" with Gordon Boelzner as our pianist. His music was light compared to the heavier classical music played at the school. We proceeded through the barre work as Balanchine indicated what he wanted us to do. He would walk about the room, occasionally pausing to stand in front of a dancer and watch. Sometimes he gave a correction. There were three other new members taking class along with me at this time. He never said anything to us; he just observed.

After class I had several hours of rehearsals with Rosemary Dunleavy, who was still dancing with the company as well as assisting Una Kai in teaching new members. The first ballet I rehearsed was the fourth movement of *Symphony in C*, with music by Bizet. Balanchine had choreographed this ballet for the Paris Opera Ballet in 1947 with Tamara Toumanova as the leading ballerina in the second-movement adagio. At that time the ballet was called *Le Palais de Cristal*, and since then it has become a mainstay of City Ballet's repertory as well as other companies. The fourth movement is short and fast and leads into the finale of the ballet. It was not easy to dance because of the fast footwork required in the *pas de bourrée* combinations of movements. I was to learn my part along with two other dancers and then rehearse later on with the rest of the company.

On the break I went downstairs to sign a contract for the season with Betty Cage, who was the company manager. She told us that we would be rehearsing one week in New York, followed by a week of performances in Toronto, Canada. I made arrangements to room with Lisa, who was also a new member, at a hotel near the theater.

My next rehearsal was for the "Emeralds" section of *Jewels*. At its premier in 1967 *Jewels* became an immediate audience favorite. It is a full-length plotless ballet with exquisite costumes by Karinska representing three gemstones. "Emeralds," with music by Fauré, is danced in a slow and smooth style. "Rubies," with music by Stravinsky, is bouncy, fast, and flashy by contrast, and "Diamonds," with music by Tchaikovsky, is classical, creating a dazzling finish. "Emeralds" is the opening section, and I was to make my debut in this ballet. The rest of the rehearsal period was devoted to *Swan Lake*, taught by Una Kai, and *La*

44

Sonambula, which was taught by John Taras, who was a co–ballet master.

My knee injury had never really gone away, and by the end of the week my knee had become very painful and swollen. The pressure of rehearsing four hours a day as well as class was just too much for it. I was very anxious as I boarded the plane for Toronto, and my worst fears came true. During the rehearsal for opening night I felt as though my knee was going to burst and realized that I would not be able to perform. In tears I went to speak to Violette Verdy about it. She was one of the principal dancers in the ballet and seemed to be a sympathetic person, someone I could turn to. She advised me to tell Rosemary so that I could be replaced for the evening. I was not destined to make my debut after all. Instead I spent the rest of the week in my hotel room taking five baths per day. When I returned to New York I saw a doctor who told me to take two weeks off. Although I had not torn anything, my knee was extremely inflamed and it would take two years before it would really ease up. Two weeks later I finally made my debut in "Emeralds" and was exhilarated by the performance in spite of my knee.

Around this time company class had become very overcrowded and Balanchine decided that newer dancers should take their morning class with Suki Schorer in the practice room, a small studio on the fifth floor, while the rest of the company took class with him. Suki was making a transition from a performing career to teaching at SAB, and I believe he thought that it would be good experience for her and better for us. Although Suki was a good teacher, I was frustrated with the situation. I had not worked all these years to get into the company to work with Suki. I wanted to dance for Balanchine, but I understood what he was trying to do. After a while the class was discontinued and we were allowed to rejoin company class.

During this time Balanchine was choreographing a new ballet that was to have its premiere during the season. Actually, he was adding three new sections to an old ballet, *Theme and Variations*, and the new ballet was called *Suite No. 3*, with music by Tchaikovsky. I was an understudy for the "Elegy" section. It was danced in bare feet, and Balanchine wanted the girls to wear their hair down. Being the consummate musician that he was, Balanchine was thoroughly familiar with the score of the music before coming to the studio. He knew exactly how many dancers he wanted to use and had decided on the structure and form that the ballet was to take. It was just a matter of making up the steps. This he did a little at a time, stopping to review what he had done. If he was satisfied, he would continue to make new movements. If it did not look right to him or if a step that he had suggested to a dancer seemed awkward to do, he would change it. His manner was calm and quiet. He did not seem to notice people going in and out of the studio, and if there was any noise it did not disturb his concentration. When rehearsal was over Balanchine sometimes jokingly said that he had to work on union time. Since all of the dancers belonged to the AGMA union there was only a certain amount of hours that they could work. Thus, the choreographer had to be creative within a set schedule of time. I loved *Elegy* and was soon afterward put into the ballet, replacing a dancer who was shifted to another section.

It was the annual *Nutcracker* time again. Because I was tall I was a parent in the party scene in the first act. I danced in "Snowflakes," a number at the end of the first act, and in the second act I danced in "Waltz of the Flowers." The party scene was a lot of fun. I had four kids (students from the children's division at SAB), and I liked my partner who played my husband. We had the freedom to talk onstage because the orchestra played so loudly that the audience could not hear us. Later on during the month, Ronald Bates, who was the production manager, told everyone to tone it down because we were getting carried away. "Snowflakes" was beautiful to watch out front, but in reality it was treacherous to dance. One had to be careful to avoid the spongy debris leftover from the soldiers and mice scene. Stagehands dropped so much paper snow on us that it was literally like dancing in the snow, and sometimes conditions could be hazardous. Fortunately, I had an alternate for "Snowflakes," but I had to dance every single performance of "Waltz of the Flowers." This number built stamina, but it was exhausting as well. During the month my body reached such a high level of exhaustion that there were times when it felt like lead.

In January the company returned to regular repertory and I learned and performed *Stars and Stripes*, with music by Sousa. Since I was the only new dancer being put in the tall girls' section of the ballet, my rehearsals were private with Una Kai. She worked me very hard, and I tried to the best of my ability to measure up despite the enormous pain of my injured knee. I did not let my injury spoil my enthusiasm and joy of performing the ballet onstage. I had grown up watching *Stars and Stripes* and now was dancing in the very ballet that had inspired me. When Balanchine came to this country he was intrigued with the idea of choreographing ballets using American themes. *Stars and Strips, Western Symphony*, and *Who Cares*, the last to the tunes of Gershwin, were very popular, appealing to a wide audience. Violette Verdy and Helgi Tomasson were often paired together in *Stars and Stripes*. Both were superb dancers with fine technique, line, and style.

The season ended in the middle of February with a

week of performances of *Don Quixote*, a full-length production in three acts, choreographed in 1965 to a commissioned score by Nabokov. Kay Mazzo danced the leading role of Dulcinea, which had originally been choreographed for Suzanne Farrell. Kay was a beautiful dancer. She had moved up through the ranks of the company and was given many of Suzanne's roles when she left. Unfortunately, there was very little dancing for tall girls in this production. I was a peasant in the first act and in the second act, as a lady of the court, I made an entrance in a long black dress with a hoopskirt, a tall black velvet hat, white ruffled collar, and three-inch high heels. After dancing the "Sarabande" with my partner, I remained standing onstage while other dancers performed for Don Quixote, Sancho Panza, and the royalty. Balanchine was never satisfied with his original production and subsequently expanded the first act by adding a dancing section, which I eventually performed. I remember seeing Balanchine perform the role of the Don with Suzanne Farrell when I was a student. It was unusual for him to appear onstage, and I found it fascinating to watch him. Although it was not a dancing role, his performance was dramatic and moving in his portrayal of the Don and his homage to ideal womanhood.

We had six weeks off and I went to the unemployment insurance office once a week on Ninetieth Street and Broadway, where I bumped into other company members. My father had retired from the business because of his health and was using his time to develop his skills in oil painting. My mother, who had a part-time job, took a month off so that they could make a trip to the south of France, staying with friends who had a villa there. They took many photographs of the scenic views of the Riviera, and when they returned home, my father made paintings from the slides. The friends my parents had stayed with happened to be the aunt and uncle of the now famous composer Andrew Lloyd Webber. When he was in New York working on his production of *Jesus Christ Superstar*, he contacted my parents and came to dinner at our apartment with his lyricist, Tim Rice. They gave us the album of *Joseph and the Amazing Technicolor Dreamcoat*, which was the first show they had put on in London. We thought they were very personable and talented but did not realize then what an enormously successful career Webber would eventually have. A year later his brother Julian Webber, who was a concert cellist, also visited us.

Although I had time off to rest, it did not seem to help my injury very much, as my knee remained stiff and swollen. I suppose I could have considered quitting, but the thought never occurred to me. I was just at the beginning of my career, and I wanted to dance. I decided to do a barre every day at home in preparation for the coming season. A dancer's body gets out of condition very easily when one stops working. The more time one takes off, the longer it takes to get back into shape.

In the spring we had a lengthy rehearsal period prior to the performing season. This time was needed to rehearse the repertory and prepare new works. I learned the first movement of *Western Symphony* and *Concerto No. 2*, by Tchaikovsky. These would be the last rehearsals with Una, because she was leaving and Rosemary would be taking her place. *Concerto No. 2*, formerly called *Ballet Imperial*, was not only undergoing a name change, but its costumes were being changed as well. Instead of wearing classical tutus, the girls would be costumed in flowing chiffon. During my first rehearsal Una came up to me and whispered that she wanted me to dance the rehearsal full out so that I would get stronger. Some of the other dancers had been marking the steps (not dancing full out) and I had been marking them, too, in order to protect my knee, which was bothering me. I was so astonished by what Una said that I immediately started dancing full out as if I were performing. After this incident I never attempted to mark a rehearsal again.

Balanchine was choreographing a new ballet called *Pamtgg,* (named for the slogan: "Pan Am makes the going great") which was to have its premier in June. Unfortunately, it turned out to be a flop. It was a learning experience for me, however, because I had the opportunity to work with Balanchine directly as he choreographed it on us. We ended the season with a week of performances of *A Midsummer Night's Dream*, a full-length ballet in two acts. My father told me that he had sold Balanchine the piano score for the ballet when he was choreographing it in 1962. It is one of the few story ballets in the repertory. Balanchine added his mastery to Shakespeare and Mendelssohn to create a beautiful and delightful ballet that captured the wit, humor, and fantasy of the Shakespearean tale. Since I was a new member, I was a hound in the first act and I danced in the "Wedding March" in the second act.

During July we performed at the Saratoga Performing Arts Center. Lisa and I took a room together again at the Rip Van Dam Motel, where I had stayed the year before as an apprentice. We were both somewhat depressed, because she had bursitis of her big toe and my knee still troubled me. Instead of eating out we bought a two-burner electric stove and cooked in, feasting on hamburgers, steaks, eggs, etc. Although it was against the rules to swim in the outdoor motel pool at night, Lisa, Colleen, and I used to sneak downstairs to go for a midnight swim after the performance. Looking back on it now, I don't know how we found the energy to do those laps on top of the strenuous days and evenings we put in at the theater.

After Saratoga we flew to Chicago. We were performing at Ravinia, outside the city. Upon arriving at O'Hare Airport, we were bussed to Evanston, where we had accommodations. The best that can be said for this tour was that our room included a fully equipped kitchen, so we didn't have to bring our stove with us. When I turned the television on, I got Walter Cronkite and the world news at six o'clock because we were on central time. In New York it came on at seven o'clock and I never got to watch it because I had to be at the theater.

As a general rule, when we were on tour during the summer Rosemary arranged the schedule so that we were through with class and rehearsals by three o'clock. We usually returned to the hotel for a dinner break and then went back to the theater to put on our makeup, warm up, and perform. In New York it was different because we could rehearse up to five o'clock and still be expected to perform in the first ballet. Under these circumstances, I would remain at the theater, taking a shower and eating a light dinner I had brought from home. After the performance I ate another meal.

Food was never a problem for me. As a child I ate everything and liked everything. By the time I was taking class every day at SAB, I realized that it was important to eat well in order to dance well. Certain foods gave me strength and energy, and other foods were a drag on the system. I ate meat, vegetables, salad, and fruit. My one vice was ice cream. Many dancers in the company drank soda. I preferred tea with honey, because it felt more digestible to dance on. I suppose there were some dancers who dieted, but it was not necessary. If one ate sensibly, one burned off the calories through strenuous exercise.

In the fall there were teaching rehearsals of *Serenade*, the "Diamonds" section of *Jewels, Scotch Symphony*, and

Episodes. We learned Frederick Ashton's *Illuminations* and Antony Tudor's *Dim Lustre*. There were certain ballets that newer dancers performed and other ballets that they understudied. For example, one had to wait several years to be put into *Serenade*, but if the person one understudied was out with an injury or an illness one got to perform it sooner. It was important to be prepared, as I would soon discover.

One evening during the season I had finished a performance of "Emeralds" and was preparing to go home. I was in the dressing room, a large room on the fourth floor where the newer dancers had their places. There was a long table with individual mirrors and lights. Each dancer had her own theater case, which was kept against the wall under the coatrack. There was a connecting door leading to a smaller room, which senior corps dancers used. The door happened to be open, and suddenly I saw Donna standing there in her "Diamonds" costume. I was her understudy. She had danced the waltz, and when she saw me she told me that she wasn't feeling well and did not think she could go on for the polonaise and the finale. Although I already had my coat on, I saw no alternative but to offer to do it for her. I changed into her costume as quickly as I could, with Donna hooking me up. Fortunately, I still had my tights on and my hair up. I just had to put my point shoes and the headpiece on. I made a mad dash for the elevator, which took me to the stage level, where I raced into the wings and found my partner, Nolan T'Sani, who was wondering where Donna was. We just had a few moments to go over the opening steps of the polonaise, and I made my debut in "Diamonds" with a smile on my face and no makeup. Nolan was a gallant partner as he guided me graciously about the stage, and I had no trouble remembering the steps. When the curtain came down and we took our bows,

I felt proud of myself. I had risen to the challenge, but was a little sorry that I had to do it without any makeup on.

Danilova was invited to stage *Les Sylphides* for the company, which was to premier in February as *Chopiniana*. When I danced this ballet three years before in the workshop Balanchine may have already been thinking of doing it for the company. Instead of wearing costumes, we performed in white leotards with skirts. It did not go over very well and was soon removed from the repertory. Perhaps it was the lack of costuming or that it was too old-fashioned.

When the season was over there was a short layoff, after which we resumed rehearsals for the spring season. The first time Balanchine acknowledged my association with the Patelson Music House was during a rehearsal of a new ballet he was choreographing for the Stravinsky Festival. He wanted the girls to form a diagonal line in order of our height from the tallest girl downstage to the shortest upstage. It took some time to accomplish this because we had to compare ourselves with each other. I measured to be fourth from the tall end of the line. Sometimes Balanchine would make a humorous remark during rehearsal or in class, and from the expression on his face it looked as if he was going to say something unusual. Suddenly he asked each dancer what the name of the music was that he was using. Caught off guard, they stared at him with a blank expression, unable to answer.

When it was my turn, I said, "Symphony in Three Movements."

Balanchine replied, "You would know. You sell the music."

We performed the ballet on opening night of the festival, and it was hailed as a major work, indicating a resurgence of Balanchine's creative drive. It was modern in style, with sharp and angular movements. We wore white leotards with belts and our hair in high pony tails. When the curtain was raised we dazzled the audience with a stream-lined effect as we stood posed in the diagonal before executing the first movements of the ballet.

The Stravinsky Festival opened on June 18, 1972, celebrating what would have been the composer's ninetieth birthday. Stravinsky had passed away the previous year, and Balanchine wanted to honor the composer with whom he had had an enduring artistic relationship. In one week the company presented thirty-one ballets, including over twenty new works. It was an extraordinary artistic achievement. Several choreographers participated along with Balanchine, including Robbins, Taras, Bolender, Clifford, Tanner, and Massine. Throughout the entire rehearsal period up until curtain time there was a heightened sense of excitement and energy. Balanchine and Kirstein made a rare appearance together when they came onstage in front of the curtain to drink a toast to Stravinsky, and the audience loved it.

In addition to *Symphony in Three Movements* I danced in several other ballets, including Taras's *Scene de Ballet* and *Song of the Nightingale*, works by Clifford and Tanner, and Balanchine's *Scherzo à la Russe, Pulcinella, Orpheus*, and *Choral Variations on Bach's Vom Himmel Hoch*. In *Scherzo à la Russe* we surprised the audience because the ballet was so short, lasting only a few minutes. It was a charming ballet just for girls, performed in white dresses, with Kay Mazzo and Karin Von Aroldingin as the leading dancers. In *Orpheus* I danced as a bacchante. The movements required a strong attack. At one point I had to stand in front of the two soloists, Jean-Pierre Bonnefous and Gloria Govrin, as they fell toward me, bearing quite a bit of their weight. I had hurt my back in another rehearsal, pulling a muscle in my upper back and neck. Although it was a very painful condition, I could dance with it, but the pressure of their weight was too much. Donna, who happened to dance next to me, offered to change places when I told her of my problem so that she could bear the weight and I could stand on the side, supporting Jean-Pierre's arm, which was easier. I was grateful to Donna. That was the beginning of a back problem that was to become more serious later on.

There were two other ballets choreographed by Balanchine that were acknowledged as impressive masterworks. These were *Violin Concerto* and *Duo Concertant*. I was an understudy for *Violin Concerto* and was later put into the ballet. The leading dancers were Kay Mazzo, Peter Martins, Karin Von Aroldingin, and Jean-Pierre Bonnefous. Balanchine made an exquisite pas de deux for each couple. This ballet was a brilliant visual counterpart to the music. The festival demonstrated that Balanchine was still at the peak of his creative and productive powers and that the company had reached its highest standard of excellence.

We returned to Saratoga for the summer season, and this time I took a single room on the ground level of the motel, which proved to be a great mistake. One night after a performance I was in bed fast asleep when I was rudely awakened by a rattling noise at my door. Someone was trying to get into my room. In a panic, I hurriedly phoned the reception desk. Then I put on my robe and, grabbing a fruit knife and a catsup bottle, stood waiting behind the door ready to defend myself. The night clerk was quick at flashing a spotlight across the parking lot in the direction of my door, and the noise stopped. Apparently the culprit had been scared off. A few minutes later the night clerk knocked at my door to see if I was all right. The next day I moved to a room on the second level. In retrospect, it makes me shudder to think of what might have happened and I consider myself to have been extremely lucky.

On my day off, I usually spent time at the pool and on one occasion ran into Ted, who was a dancer with the company. He had been flirting with me in New York. I first noticed his attention when I became aware that he was looking at me repeatedly in class and rehearsals. So far he had not asked me out. There were very few single available men in the company. Many of the men were homosexuals, and those who were not were already married or had girlfriends. There was not much time for a social life outside the theater because of the demand of the schedule and the discipline of the work.

After swimming and talking for some time, Ted and I parted company. Of course I saw him almost daily at the theater. He continued his flirtatious behavior toward me, but still he did not ask me out. A couple of weeks later, when Lisa and I were in Friendly's having some ice cream, Ted came in. When he saw us he came over and sat down. It seemed to me that he took an awfully long time to decide what he wanted, then finally ordered a black-and-white soda. This was the beginning of a friendship that would prove to be a frustration for me.

After Saratoga we repeated another week at Ravinia performing some of the Stravinsky Festival ballets. During the week I developed a terrible case of hay fever and was always afraid of having a sneezing fit onstage. This time we stayed in Chicago, but because of my condition, when I was not at the theater I spent a good deal of my time indoors at the hotel ordering room service.

In the middle of August the company flew to Munich, where we performed at the Staatsoper Theater. It was the week before the opening of the Olympic games. Munich had an old-world charm retained when it was rebuilt in its original style after it was destroyed during the bombings of World War II. The theater was large and elegant. During our stay we were invited to a formal dinner given by the consul general of the United States in honor of our visit. It was my first formal occasion, and I felt sophisticated in a long pink dress with my hair up in a French twist and wearing the cultured pearl earrings my parents had given me. The event was held at the theater, where there was a reception on the promenade followed by a dinner downstairs where tables were set up. When I came into the dining area I saw that Ted was sitting with another dancer and some other guests. I had no intention of sitting down with them, but the other dancer encouraged me to join them, so I did. I knew that Ted was dating her because I had accidentally overheard her talking about him in the dressing room. I was not jealous; in fact, I liked her. I was annoyed with Ted. When the dinner was over he took me home in a cab because we were staying at the same hotel. She was staying at another hotel.

Since my schedule was not very heavy, I had time to do some sightseeing, including a trip to the site of the Olympic Games. Only a few dancers showed up for this tour, including Ted and myself. It was an opportunity to spend some time with him, but he was in a very uncommunicative mood and it was not much fun. The only thing we accomplished was that he took a picture of me for my photo album, but by then I was out of sorts. A week later, after we returned home, the world was stunned by the assassination of the Israeli Olympic athletes by Arab terrorists.

Chapter 6
Dancing in Russia

In 1962, after a thirty-eight-year absence, Balanchine made a triumphant return to Russia with the New York City Ballet. Ten years later, the company was making a second visit. Some of the older dancers who had gone on the first trip warned new members that we should bring along such items as drain stoppers, toilet paper, and canned food. I paid heed to their warning and packed a supply bag containing seven cans of tuna fish, ten packs of peanut butter crackers, one round vinyl drain stopper, plenty of toilet paper and Kleenex, and a small pot for boiling water with a converter plug, as well as a jar of Taster's Choice coffee.

Our tour was sponsored by the Department of State under the Cultural Presentations Program. Several members of the State Department accompanied us. Relations between the Soviet Union and the United States were good at this time. On a beautiful day in September the company boarded Pan Am at Kennedy Airport and flew to Kiev, capital of the Ukraine. After a ten-hour flight we made a smooth landing and were behind the Iron Curtain. As we were preparing to disembark, Balanchine was standing at the front of the cabin and I noticed that he had a very special expression on his face. I think he was proud of the company and to be bringing his American dancers to his homeland for a second time. A stairway was brought to our plane, and positioned on the tarmac some distance from the terminal. Balanchine led the way down, and we followed him. On the ground he was greeted officially. Afterward we all trooped to the terminal to have our passports stamped and board buses for our hotel, which was about a half an hour away. Along the way the sights were drab and I saw women doing heavy roadwork, digging ditches. Upon arriving at the hotel, we were served lunch in a large dining room. The food was not very appetizing, giving us an indication of what we might expect during the tour. There was a woman attendant on each floor who held the keys to our rooms. The first thing I noticed about my room was that there was a radio with only one station that could not be turned off, only lowered in volume. There was a bathtub but, as predicted, no drain stopper in the sink, and the brown toilet paper was harsh. I was very glad to see my luggage arrive a little later and especially to see my supply bag.

For this tour we had to have a roommate. I had hoped that Lisa would be available because we had gotten along well before, but she was rooming with someone else. Instead I roomed with a newer girl in the company whom I did not know very well. Later when it was time to go to dinner I asked her if she would be going downstairs, but she declined, saying she was going to skip the meal. I was concerned for her, but I did not feel that it was my business to say anything. When I walked into the dining room most of the tables were taken. I saw that Ted was sitting with Frank Ohman, who was a soloist, and there was an extra seat at their table, so I decided to sit down with them. It seemed like the logical thing to do considering the rapport I had with Ted. John Taras, who happened to be sitting at the next table, raised his glass and toasted me, and I in turn toasted him. I enjoyed working with John and felt that he liked my work. He taught company class when Balanchine did not. I was twenty years old now and feeling more relaxed socially in the company. My knee had eased up considerably, and I was dancing better because of this.

The food turned out to be a great disappointment for the entire Russian tour. Part of the problem was that we were served as a group and unable to order what we wanted. They served poor-quality meat, chicken, and potatoes, with no salad or fruit. The bread was coarse and the ice cream had a grainy texture. There was only one beverage on the table, lemon soda. We were told not to drink the water, and the only time I did was when I boiled it in the pot that I had brought with me. Many of the dancers came down with intestinal problems during the tour, but fortunately, I never had any trouble. My Central American experience held me in good stead, helping me to be adaptable and flexible about food.

The next day our toilet broke down. I happened to meet Madame Molostwoff, who was accompanying us on the trip, and told her about it. She wrote a note in Russian for me to give the attendant on my floor, and the toilet was subsequently fixed by a woman plumber.

The company performed at the Ukraina Palace of Culture, a new and modern theater that seated 3,800 people. Robert Irving and Hugo Fiorato alternated in conducting the sixty-member Soviet orchestra that accompanied us throughout the tour. Tickets were sold out in advance. The audience was eager to be pleased. The opening night program consisted of *Serenade*, with music by Tchaikovsky, *Scherzo Fantastique*, with music by Stravinsky, a Robbins ballet, Stravinsky's *Violin Concerto*, and Gershwin's *Who Cares*. The Russians were used to story ballets, and the abstract style of Balanchine and Robbins was at first received with some reserve. The Russians had a special way of applauding, in rhythmic hand clapping, which grew stronger throughout the evening. They especially liked the *Violin Concerto*; Stravinsky's music was rarely performed in Russia. *Who Cares*, with the American music of Gershwin, was given rousing applause. During the final curtain calls Robert Irving called upon the young Soviet musician who had played the violin solo for the Stravinsky to take a bow, and at the end Balanchine was presented with a huge flowerpot as he bowed to a standing ovation. During the week I danced in *Symphony in C* and "Elegy" in *Suite No. 3*. We presented "Diamonds" from *Jewels* and three other works by Robbins, including *Dances at a Gathering*, to the music of Chopin, *Goldberg Variations*, and *Dumbarton Oaks*.

One morning I was standing outside in front of the hotel chatting with Colleen and Lisa while waiting for the bus to the theater. Balanchine, who happened to be nearby, invited us to go for a walk up the block. No sooner had we gotten started than we all found ourselves tongue-tied. I then thought to question him about his homeland. He enjoyed being the educator, and we listened attentively. I was able to respond to what he was saying and asked another question. It was the first time I had had a lengthy conversation with him. When I got in the company I was so in awe of Balanchine that it would have been difficult to talk to him, but now it did not seem to be a problem.

The company was given a tour of the city. They showed us many churches, which surprised me, because religion was not encouraged in the Soviet Union. I brought my camera along, and although we were permitted to photograph the churches, we were not permitted to photograph a couple of other sights.

After a week in Kiev the company flew to Leningrad (formerly and now called Saint Petersburg), in the northern part of Russia. Balanchine had been born here. Leningrad was a beautiful city with pastel-colored buildings, wide boulevards, and the Neva River, with its canals and bridges. Although it was only the end of September, it was extremely cold. The theater was some distance away from the center of the city. Here the conditions were not good. There was no heat, the dressing rooms were crowded, and the stage floor was particularly unacceptable. We were traveling with our own gray linoleum flooring, making it possible for us to dance. The stage was raked (slanted), not uncommon in Europe, and we had to adjust our bodies to it.

We were invited to demonstrate a company class at the Kirov Ballet School (formerly Imperial School). Balanchine had been a student at the school, and he remarked how little everything had changed. Ballet in Russia had stayed much the same because the state discouraged Western influence in the arts.

After we gave our demonstration, the teachers gathered around while Balanchine explained his ideas. They were impressed by the fast tempo in which we danced. The Russians dance in a slower, measured style. We were given tickets for a performance of the Kirov Ballet Company at the Maryinsky Theater, where Balanchine was once a member. The young and talented Baryshnikov was dancing, and he impressed us tremendously. Afterward backstage I overheard Peter Martins, a principal dancer in our company, encouraging Baryshnikov to defect to the West. Two years later he did, following Nureyev and Makarova.

There was one very unpleasant and disturbing incident that occurred at the theater when we were rehearsing. A young Russian fan who had followed us from Kiev was forcibly taken by the state police. Russian citizens were not free to travel from city to city without a permit, and it was evident that the government did not approve of friendly contact with Westerners.

After our success in Leningrad, we flew south to Tbilisi in Georgia. It took five hours on the Russian airline Aeroflot. This was an uncomfortable flight particularly because of the air compression in the cabin, which was painful to my ears. The only food served was an apple and a hard roll. Candy was given out on takeoff and landing, which helped to relieve the pressure.

Tbilisi was warm and balmy, with a strong Mediterranean influence. There were very few women to be seen on the streets. We attracted a great deal of attention and because the dancers were approached so often by groups of men, we were bussed from the hotel to the theater even though it was within walking distance.

Balanchine's ancestors were from Georgia and his brother, Andrei Balanchivadze, a well-established symphonic composer, lived there. During an intermission at one of the performances Balanchine was quoted as saying, "All of a sudden I have millions of relatives. Every time I turn around they are introducing me to this one, and introducing me to that one. People I never knew were relatives appear. More than the last time we were here."

We were given a banquet with entertainment by the exhilarating Georgian dancers and singers. Balanchine and his brother made speeches toasting each other and the company. This was a very special occasion, and I found it moving to see the two brothers together. Audiences were wildly enthusiastic. On the last night, which was a sellout, we heard that hundreds of people gate-crashed, forcing their way into the theater, standing in the aisles, sitting two in one seat, and filling every available space. With Georgian hospitality and the overwhelming response of the audience, Tbilisi was the high point of the tour.

In Moscow we stayed in a very large modern hotel centrally located near Red Square, the Church of Saint

Basil, and Lenin's Tomb. Nearby behind the Kremlin walls was our theater among the magnificent picturesque cathedrals with their gilded domes and the palaces of the czars that were now museums housing the national treasures. I was given an official pass with my name written in Russian. We performed in the Hall of Congress, a massive theater that seated 6,000. The stage was huge. In "Elegy" I had to exit on the right side and soon afterward make an entrance from the left. The hallway behind the stage seemed endless as I ran from one side to the other, barely making it on time.

The company was invited to give a demonstration at the Bolshoi Ballet School. Balanchine gave a class and we did a runthrough of *Violin Concerto*. I got to dance the ballet for the first time, replacing another dancer who was ill. The Bolshoi School put on a demonstration for us. Selected students from the very youngest to the most advanced performed. I particularly enjoyed watching the younger students, who were more expressive and livelier than the older ones.

During the week the Soviet minister of culture hosted a luncheon for the company. I recall walking into a room where there was a receiving line. Balanchine introduced me to some Russians, and I shook hands with them. Then Balanchine, pretending to be on the receiving line, shook my hand, smiling at me. He had a funny sense of humor.

In Moscow I felt free to walk on the streets and was less conspicuous. I shopped on the well-known Gorki Street and in Gum, the big department store. We were given tickets to the Moscow Circus, which was great fun. I happened to have a seat next to Jacques D'Amboise. When I was a little girl watching him perform at City Center I never dreamed that years later I would be seeing the circus with him, in Russia of all places!

We spent almost one month in the Soviet Union. The people were friendly, and the audiences were very responsive. The most overt sign of Communism was the display of Lenin in all the buildings and on the streets and monuments wherever we went.

The final week of our tour was in Poland, in the cities of Lodz and Warsaw. On our way from Lodz to Warsaw by bus we stopped off to see the birthplace of Chopin. In Warsaw I felt there was a more Western European influence. The food was much better, and we were able to order what we wanted. I thought I recognized cauliflower on the menu and ordered it. When the waiter brought my dinner it seemed as if he served me a whole head of cauliflower. A little embarrassed, I tried to eat it quickly to get rid of it.

The theaters in Lodz and Warsaw were smaller than the huge theaters in the Soviet Union. There was more contact with the audience, and they received us warmly. *Dances at a Gathering* was especially appreciated because Chopin was revered as a national hero. On our last night, in an interview at the National Theater in Warsaw, Balanchine said of his company's tour, "I'm glad we were able to do this. Europeans feel that we can only build machines and automobiles. They think we have no soul." Before leaving Poland, Balanchine left our stage floor as a gift for the Polish Ballet Company, autographing it in one corner. Subsequently they cut out the place he had autographed, framed it, and hung it in the Polish Ballet School. It had been a triumphant tour, but I was exhausted and grateful to return to the uninhibited freedom of my own country.

Chapter 7
Choreography

There were only about three weeks of rehearsals before the winter season would be opening in November. We had to wait for the City Opera to vacate the dressing rooms before we could move in. I had spent two years in the large dressing room and wanted to move into the smaller one. I knew there would be a vacancy in that room because one of the dancers had left the company. I put my name on a piece of paper and left it on one of the places to reserve it. Soon afterward I was approached by one of the dancers who had been in that dressing room for several years. She told me that they wanted another dancer to move in instead of me. I was put off by her unfriendly manner, but I just said I was tired of being in the big room and wanted a change. When I saw the other dancer I told her what had happened and asked her if she wanted to move into that room. She was surprised and said she had no intention of moving in there. I decided to move in because it was a matter of principle. I wasn't going to allow a few dancers to control the dressing room that way. After I moved in, all was forgotten and everyone was friendly and accepted my presence there.

On my day off I often listened to music at home. We had a large record collection. I became interested in the Brahms Trio no. 2 in C Major, op. 87, and thought it would make a good ballet. I went to see my uncle at the Music House to get the score of the music so that I could study it. It was a piano trio for piano, violin, and cello. I decided to use twenty-two dancers. There would be eleven dancers in the first movement, two leading dancers and nine in the corps de ballet forming three trios, with two girls and a boy in each trio. In the second movement there would be three couples and a leading couple, and in the third movement there would be a trio for two boys and a girl. The fourth movement would be a finale with all of the dancers. I envisioned the musicians onstage with the dancers as they performed the ballet. I began choreographing on myself and writing the steps down in a notebook. When I got in the company I made it a habit to write down all the ballets that I learned. I found that it helped me to retain the material better. I also thought that if I ever wanted to teach the ballets, my notes would be invaluable. Now, since I could not work with the dancers in the studio the way Balanchine did, I envisioned the ballet while making up the steps. I also kept in mind certain dancers and their abilities. For example, when I choreographed the trio for the third movement, I thought of Bart Cook, Victor Castelli, and Colleen Neary. I was aware of how other dancers danced, their capabilities, and the style in which they moved. I observed company members in class and rehearsals and watched performances from the wings when I wasn't dancing.

It took me one month to complete the ballet simultaneously while we were performing the *Nutcracker*. I wanted to speak to Balanchine about it but felt a little timid, so I went to Violette Verdy for advice. She was very supportive and enthusiastic and encouraged me to talk to Balanchine. One evening during a performance he was sitting backstage next to the supply table. There was another chair nearby and I thought that this was the perfect opportunity to talk to him, so I went over and sat down. I told him about my ballet, mentioning the music that I was using. His manner was matter-of-fact and he made no comment about the music, but he suggested that usually one started by going to the school and working with the students or one could work with friends.

After thinking it over, I decided not to go to the school, because I was unfamiliar with the students. It seemed more logical to ask friends, since I had already choreographed parts of the ballet with company members in mind. I asked Colleen, Bart, and Victor if they would work with me, explaining that they would not have to stand while I thought up the steps, because I had prepared the material ahead of time. I told them that I wanted to show it to Balanchine when we were ready. They were very receptive and agreed to rehearse. After they had learned and danced it for me, it was exciting to see that it looked good. I did not feel that I had to make any changes. I asked Dan Duell to work with me on the second-movement adagio, and he also was willing to give me his time. I had made a variation on myself and one for him that suited his abilities. Francis and Paul rehearsed another section of the movement, and I saw that it needed to be changed. I found dancers to learn the first movement and saw that some of it looked good and some of it needed to be revised. I was very grateful to all the dancers for giving me their time and energy. It was a fantastic learning experience for me. I had told Rosemary Dunleavy about the project and asked her to give me any available time and studio space, and she was more than willing to help out. I think that many members of the company became aware of what I was doing.

Finally I was ready to show Balanchine the trio for Colleen, Bart, and Victor. I decided against demonstrating myself because I didn't think it was right to dance and direct at the same time. During a performance, Balanchine was standing in the first wing on stage right, where he usually watched when he was not out front. I went up to him and told him what I had prepared, mentioning the three dancers I was using. I asked him if he would look at it. His response was, "What is the rush? It is not like a newspaper deadline." My heart sank. I was shocked and disturbed. There seemed to be a finality in his manner as he said this to me. I did not want to anger him by persisting. I was still very new in the company and felt I could not say anything further about it.

I thought of asking Rosemary to look at my work so that she could speak to Balanchine on my behalf, but it seemed as if I might be putting her in an awkward position so I changed my mind. I thought of going to Jerome Robbins and asking him to look at it but decided against the idea. I tried hard to analyze what Balanchine had said to me. There was a message in what he had said. This could wait for some future time when I was more mature. He wanted me to concentrate on my dancing now. When I first talked to him about the project and he had suggested that I use friends it never occurred to me that he would refuse to look at my work. In the end I was forced to shelve it and wait for better timing. Perhaps if I moved up in the company he would be more receptive at a later date.

During the season I was shifted from the fourth movement of *Symphony in C* to the third movement and enjoyed dancing it very much. The costumes for the ballet were white tutus for the girls and black tops and tights for the boys. After years of use, the tutus were worn out and needed to be replaced. I was scheduled for a fitting at Karinska's on West Fifty-seventh Street. Karinska had designed costumes for many of Balanchine's ballets. When the tutus arrived and I put mine on, it turned out to be a disaster.

The upper part was so snug that I could hardly breathe during the performance. Madame Pourmel had to give me another costume to wear, and I was so disappointed that I could not wear the one that had been custom-made for me.

When the season was over we had the usual layoff, but I was not content to rest and took classes with Peter Nelson who had his own school. Around this time Sally had made plans to go to Bermuda with a friend and invited me to join them. I hadn't had a real vacation in a long time, so her offer sounded appealing. After only a few days I felt as if I had been away for weeks and came back refreshed and invigorated. When the rehearsal period started in the spring I returned to rehearse the first movement of the *Brahms-Schoenberg Quartet*. I had been performing the fourth movement. Balanchine had choreographed this ballet in 1966. I loved the music and had a recording of the original piano quartet at home. Schoenberg's stunning realization of it for orchestra and dancing Balanchine's choreography in a beautiful costume were very special for me.

Another ballet I learned and performed that season was *The Cage*, with choreography by Robbins and music by Stravinsky. The only time I had worked with Robbins was when I was an apprentice for *Firebird* monsters and when he rehearsed the *Nutcracker* one time when Balanchine was out of town. Robbins had a reputation for being difficult. I was a little apprehensive about rehearsing *The Cage* with him and not sure what to expect. I had learned the ballet with Rosemary, and this rehearsal was to be a final polishing with Robbins in the studio before rehearsing and performing it onstage.

Working with Robbins was a totally different experience than working with Balanchine. Aside from the differences in their personalities, the way in which they worked was not the same. Robbins was very precise and exacting when instructing a dancer on how to dance a movement or a series of movements. With Balanchine a dancer had more leeway. Occasionally he could be more specific, but in general one had more freedom of interpretation. During the rehearsal for *The Cage* Robbins became dissatisfied with the way the dancers were doing a series of movements and stopped the rehearsal in order to work individually with each dancer. We had to raise the knee turned in alternating legs on point while simultaneously doing a back bend with the right arm thrust forward and the hand in a position so that the palm faced upward and the thumb was stretched back, separated from the other fingers. The left arm was behind the back. He gave the same type of correction to each dancer: It was not sharp enough. There was not enough attack. It was too meek. Since I was the last dancer to do it for him, I was determined not to get the same correction. When my turn came I threw myself into the movement with such force that when it was over Robbins looked at me thoughtfully and said nothing. I think I produced what he wanted.

Melissa Hayden was retiring at the end of the season, and Balanchine was choreographing a new ballet for her in honor of the occasion. Melissa had had a very long career with the company, joining in 1949. She was a brilliant and versatile dancer, creating roles in *Divertimento No. 15* (1956), *Stars and Stripes* (1958), *Liebeslieder Waltzer* (1960), and many others. Jacques D'Amboise, who often danced with her, would be partnering her again in this ballet. It was called *Cortège Hongrois*, and Karin Von Aroldingen and Jean-Pierre Bonnefous were the leading dancers in the czardas. I was an understudy for this section and was responsible for knowing the parts of the two dancers on the right side of the stage. Another dancer was responsible for the dancers on the left. When it came time for the performance, Rose-

71

mary asked me if I could go on for one of the dancers on the left side who was injured. Apparently the understudy who was responsible was unprepared. Of course I said I would, although it meant that I would have to reverse some of the movements. It didn't bother me to jump into someone's place on short notice. I loved the challenge and went out there and enjoyed the performance.

During the summer in Saratoga, I danced several performances of *Scotch Symphony*, with music by Mendelssohn, again on short notice, because the dancer I understudied was out. This ballet, choreographed for Maria Tallchief in 1952, evokes the spirit and beauty of Scotland, with lovely costumes for the girls and colorful kilts for the men. Maria Tallchief was a wonderful dancer. I have a vivid memory of her as the Firebird, another role choreographed for her, when the company performed at City Center.

After Saratoga the company flew to California, where we were scheduled to perform at the Greek Theater in Los Angeles. Our flight was on a 747, and it was the first time I had flown on such a huge airplane. During the flight we were invited by the pilot to visit the cockpit for a fabulous aerial view.

While in LA I had time to visit a Finnish friend of my grandmother. She was elderly and sent Julie Marttila, a younger friend of hers, to pick me up at my hotel in her car. After our visit Julie gave me a tour of the area and we spent the rest of the day and evening at Disneyland. I had heard of Disneyland all my life, but I never dreamed how much fun it would turn out to be. We did all the rides, and I indulged myself in a quadruple-scoop ice cream cone. Julie worked in the administrative office of MGM and was surprised to learn that my mother had been under contract to her studio so many years ago.

I had taken a room at the Lido Hotel that included a

kitchen. On my way back from the grocery store I ran into Ted, who was also staying at the hotel, and we made a date to meet at the pool. Our relationship had remained much the same. We did not see each other outside the theater in New York, but he continued to react to me when we were in the theater. When I met him in the hall he caressed my hair, and when I ran into him in the elevator he grabbed me. These incidents took place when no one happened to be around. On another occasion, I was standing onstage very close to the wing in the village scene of *Pulcinella* when all of a sudden I felt a hand on my hand. It was Ted, standing in the wings fooling around. I never had the nerve to tell him to cut it out. Besides, I had become attracted to him.

When I arrived at the pool, Francis and Paul were there and Ronald Bates, Roland Vasquez, and a couple of other production men were sitting around a table having a beer. A few minutes later Ted arrived. I was the only female in the vicinity, and when I got up from my lounge chair and walked over to the pool in a two-piece bathing suit I could feel that every eye was upon me. Soon after, Ted joined me in the pool and we swam and chatted for a while, commiserating about our injuries. I had developed a problem with my left hip on the same leg that I had my knee injury, and Ted was having trouble with his knee. Injuries were common. They were caused by the enormous physical stress and fatigue of the work. I did discover later on, after analysis and X-rays, that I had some structural problems that contributed to my becoming chronically injured. My left leg was longer than my right, and I had a small scoliosis of my spine, which curved to the left.

We concluded the summer tour with a week at the Filene Center in the Wolftrap Farm Park, which was located in Vienna, Virginia. Being nearby, Washington was a must.

So Lisa, Colleen, and I set off to tour the White House and the Smithsonian Institute. It was my first visit to the capital, and I found it impressive and rewarding. The company was staying in a motel, and it seemed as if I had to walk miles from the main building to get to my room. In addition to this nuisance, I was kept awake night after night by a mouse rattling in my wastebasket. Finally I complained to the management. They set a trap, but this elusive mouse still kept me awake.

Taken when I was twenty-two years old *(Photo by Leyson)*

George Balanchine *(Photo courtesy of Henri-Cartier Bresson, from the New York City Ballet Souvenir Book 1975, Souvenir Book Publishers, Inc. BALANCHINE is a trademark of The George Balanchine Trust.)*

My mother, Sally, me, Dad, and Lady

Three years old, rehearsing

Practicing, age nine

In the studio in Merrick at thirteen

In the dining room

Graduating from Professional Children's School (1970)

Workshop performance of Napoli—I'm on the right (1969)

Shopping in Munich, 1972

In front of the house where I stayed in Puerto Rico, 1968

Last season, 1975 *(Photo by Leyson)*

Taken during my last season with the company *(Photo by Leyson)*

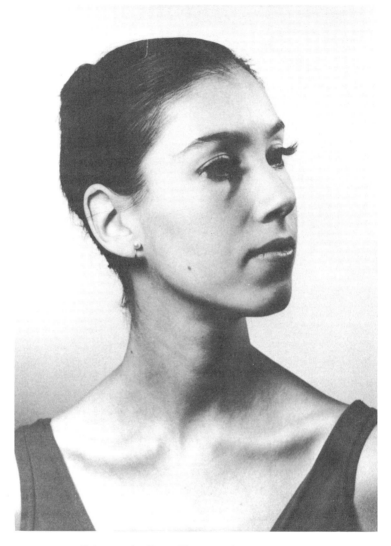

Taken at the State Theater, 1975 *(Photo by Leyson)*

Chapter 8
Filming in Berlin

In the fall of 1973 the company flew to West Berlin to film a number of ballets for European television. I was involved in five of them: *Pulcinella, Serenade, Violin Concerto*, and the finales of *Symphony in C* and *Stars and Stripes*. Some of the dancers tried to discourage the others from going, saying that the work would be grueling, with long hours and little pay. Balanchine said if we did not want to go he would find other dancers. Of course we voted to go.

On the plane going over during the middle of the flight I thought I might sit with Ted for a while. No one was sitting next to him, so I sat down, and we talked. He wanted to watch the film they were showing, but I didn't care for it. Instead I took a nap and, feeling a little romantic, rested my head on his shoulder. My slightly aggressive behavior must have disturbed him, because he stopped watching the film and made a little speech to me. I do not recall his exact words, but he was trying to express the idea that he didn't want to hurt me or be responsible or involved in a serious relationship. I listened to what he had to say and quietly returned to my own seat. When I thought it over I realized I did not appreciate his gallantry. I could not understand why he was rejecting me and what he was so afraid of, considering all the advances he had made. I also thought I would try to put the whole matter out of my mind, but this would not be easy to do, since I would be seeing him every day for the next two weeks at the film studio.

The company was located in several hotels throughout the city. I was pleasantly surprised with the room that I had, because it was large enough to accommodate a couch, a coffee table, and an armchair. It even had a terrace that faced the main thoroughfare.

After unpacking, I went across the street to a restaurant where I ran into Conrad Ludlow and Carol Sumner, who invited me to join them. Conrad, a principal dancer who was noted for his exceptional ability in partnering, would soon be leaving to direct his own company. During my stay I came to this restaurant often because of its location and the good food. However, I didn't always feel like eating out. I discovered a supermarket a couple of blocks from my hotel and shopped there regularly. Some of the foods that I was used to eating at home were packaged a little differently. For example, their can of tuna fish came with cooked peas and a sauce on top, and the fresh fruits were packed in baskets that were appealing to the eye. One time when I was checking out, the clerk became angry with me, yelling in German, causing a scene. Apparently I had given her the wrong coin. I immediately took out all my German coins and offered them so that she could choose what she wanted. Of course, she realized then that I was not German.

The film studio was about a forty-minute drive from the city. One morning when I got on the bus, I saw that there was a vacant seat in the middle of the bus. Apparently no one had the courage to sit there, because it was a side seat perpendicular to the two-seater where Balanchine was sitting with Madame Pourmel. I decided to take it. A few minutes later Balanchine became annoyed when a few dancers got on the bus carrying cups of coffee (china) that they had brought from the hotel restaurant where they had been eating breakfast. Balanchine was always very aware of the company's behavior in public, and it irritated him when the behavior was inappropriate.

I had already said, "Good morning," to Balanchine and Madame Pourmel when I sat down. As we settled into the trip I could not think of anything to say to him, but I did think of a question to ask her and soon he joined in on our conversation. Madame Pourmel had been with the company for many years and was devoted to her work. Not only was she responsible for the care of the costumes, but she often had to make alterations as well. When I was put in "Elegy" she had to practically remake the costume for me.

On my first day at the studio I had difficulty finding a dressing room. There were several small rooms, and these were filled to capacity. When I went to another area I saw Peter Martins standing in the doorway of one of the rooms. Apparently these were reserved for principal dancers. I told him of my problem, and he offered me his room, saying that he would not be filming right away and could take another room. At first I hesitated, but then I decided to take him up on his suggestion. I would be spending four weeks at this studio, and having the privacy and a peaceful place to be meant a great deal to me. There was even a cot so that I could put my feet up on the break. I was thankful to Peter for making this possible.

The first ballet we filmed was *Pulcinella*, which took two weeks to complete. It was choreographed for the Stravinsky Festival and was commedia del l'arte in style. Violette Verdy and Edward Villella had the leading roles. There was no dancing for the corps de ballet, just acting. I played the part of a townsperson. Up until now I had always done my own makeup. I had very white skin and used a light shade of pancake as a base. For the filming I had to wear a darker shade. Every morning a makeup artist applied the base and I completed the rest. My costume was short-sleeved, and while I was on the set the makeup person noticed that my arms and hands did not match my face. She rushed to apply the matching color before they shot the next take.

The dancers were often given a break when the crew needed time to make adjustments to the equipment. One time I was sitting on the floor and Ted, who had a part in this ballet, approached me, picked me up, carried me over to a chair, and put me on his lap in front of everyone, including Balanchine. I pretended to be amused as if it was a spontaneous joke, but privately I was outraged with Ted's behavior. A few days later, on our day off, Frank Ohman and I went to see a production of *My Fair Lady*. I've always loved *My Fair Lady*, going back to when I pretended to be Eliza Doolittle as a child. The lyrics I was so familiar with sounded ludicrous in German. As amusing as they were, we thoroughly enjoyed the show. Afterward Frank took me to a bistro, and while we were sitting there having some wine Ted walked in with the other dancer. When they saw us we all said hello, but they did not sit down with us. I was still angry with Ted.

The next ballet we filmed was *Serenade*. Filming a ballet for television was vastly different than a performance onstage. The ballet was not filmed as a whole but in sections. Each section was shot repeatedly from various camera angles. This was extremely fatiguing and drained the spontaneous energy that a dancer would give to a theater performance. Shooting the film covered ten hours a day, with long waiting periods between each section. This meant we had to dance cold, without a warm-up, when called upon.

Serenade, choreographed in 1934, was the first ballet Balanchine created when he came to the United States. Classic, romantic, in free-flowing costumes, it has all the beauty and freshness of the Tchaikovsky music. It took one week to film the ballet. The set looked like a stage with the cameras in front of the dancers. There happened to be a piano out front, and on one of the breaks I sat down to play. Since the breaks were long and tedious, it was boring for the dancers and I thought it would be relaxing for them to listen to some music. I played the first movement of a Mozart sonata, and when I finished I felt a hand on my shoulder. It was Balanchine, who had come over, and he said, "Thank you."

There was one section of the ballet in which I was not dancing and I sat out front to watch. After a while the dancers were standing around waiting for the crew to make some adjustments, so I took a book out of my bag to read. Balanchine, who was nearby, came over and took the book away from me, examining it to see what I was reading. It happened to be *Sister Carrie*, by Theodore Dreiser. On my day off I had gone shopping on the Kurfurstendamm and found a bookstore that sold paperbacks in English. He seemed to approve of what I was reading.

During another break Kay Mazzo and Karin Von Aroldingen were sitting on the floor in their costumes and I sat down with them to chat for a while. I felt comfortable doing this because I had a rapport with Kay. She had taken a personal interest in my work, sometimes observing me from the wings when she had time to watch. I was saying to them that Madame Pourmel would be very angry and upset if she saw us sitting on the floor in our costumes. As a general rule the dancers were not supposed to do so, and stools were provided backstage in New York for the dancers to sit on. When Balanchine saw us sitting there he came over curious to know what we were talking about. I repeated what I had said, and he smiled and nodded in agreement.

The most embarrassing incident that ever happened to me occurred during the filming of *Violin Concerto*. This ballet was performed in black leotards and skirts. While I was on a break I thought I had time to go to the bathroom, which was down the hall, and put on a pair of full-length leg warmers to keep my muscles warm. When I came back to the set I was startled to see that all of the dancers and crew and Balanchine were standing there waiting for me. I apologized profusely and tried to get out of my leg warmers as fast as I possibly could. Then they still had to wait for me to put my skirt on and tie it. Finally I made my entrance from stage right doing a fast *bourrée* opposite Colleen to Stravinsky's music. Balanchine was perfectly gracious, remaining calm and never losing his patience.

I had one week off, and instead of going to the studio to take company class, I preferred to take a barre every day in my room. My left hip, which had been bothering me, had become worse at this time. In the afternoons I went shopping and sightseeing. West Berlin was lively with theaters, movies, concert halls, cafés, and restaurants. It was affluent and the stores were well stocked with a variety of food and merchandise. I used the subway system, which was immaculate. While shopping on the Kurfurstendamm I stopped to have lunch in a restaurant. It was crowded, so the waitress seated me with some other people. They appeared to be a mother with her daughter and son, and the young man seemed to be my age. After I ordered what I wanted, we tried to communicate with each other. Since they did not speak English and I did not speak German, we all spoke French. My high school French held me in good stead. Madame Oreffice at PCS would have been proud of me. They invited me to go to a discotheque with them, but I politely declined. On another day Donna and I took a bus tour of East Berlin. In contrast to West Berlin, the East Berlin sector was drab and bleak. There were very few people on the streets. The only places we were permitted to visit were two museums. The Berlin Wall was a very depressing sight. I never dreamed that it would come down in my lifetime.

On the last week we filmed the finales of *Symphony in C* and *Stars and Stripes*. We spent six weeks in West Berlin. Filming was an exhausting experience, but it was rewarding, too. Though the films were intended for European broadcast, *Serenade* was shown on Channel 13 and I did see myself. Although the full impact of a live performance was lost on the screen, it turned out well. Later on I did receive royalties for my work.

Chapter 9
Ups and Downs

Shortly after I returned from Berlin, my parents went off to Europe to live there for an extended period of time while Sally and I shared the apartment in New York. My grandmother had found her own place when we moved from Long Island.

No sooner had my parents left than the company went on strike. There had been a rumor that the musicians were going to strike during the *Nutcracker*, and in order to prevent them from disrupting the season the dancers struck first, forcing everyone to settle their differences sooner. Three weeks later Balanchine made a speech to the company asking us to come back to work, and soon after that we did just in time for the *Nutcracker*.

During the season there were rehearsals for *Harlequinade*, which had been choreographed in 1965 on Patricia McBride and Edward Villella. When Patty and Eddie danced together they were exciting to watch, creating magic onstage not only in this ballet, but in *Tarantella* and "Rubies," which were also made for them. Balanchine wanted to expand *Harlequinade*, adding a section for the corps de ballet and the children that were used in the production. For this rehearsal he wanted everyone to gather in the back of the room so that we could make an entrance from upstage left in couples. I happened to be standing in front of the others and stayed there so that I could see clearly what he was going to do. He jumped off his right leg, raising the left leg a little forward with the knee bent. Then he turned around to watch me do it. I interpreted it to be a jump off the right leg with the left leg in *attitude* front, and I did the step full out for him, jumping higher and raising my leg higher than he had. He seemed pleased with what I did. Then he took my hand and with him facing me in a diagonal we danced it together. We did two additional small jumps (*emboités*), which I also did, and we repeated the movements starting with the other leg. Then Steve Caras, who had been standing by, took Balanchine's place and we led the line in a diagonal. We circled around as Balanchine directed us until everyone was in place. Then he continued to choreograph new movements. This was not considered an important role to dance, but what mattered was what happened in the studio with Balanchine. It was in this way that he got to know his dancers, what their capabilities were, if they were able to pick up the choreography quickly, and how they looked when they danced. What happened in class and rehearsals was equally important as what happened onstage.

When the season ended there was a short layoff followed by a week of performances at the Kennedy Center in Washington, D.C. The theater was located in an attractive setting on the Potomac River and was walking distance from the hotel. I stayed at the Howard Johnson and did my grocery shopping across the street at the Watergate Hotel, where there was a supermarket beneath the complex. We were performing *A Midsummer Night's Dream* for the entire week, and by this time I had progressed from a hound to a fairy in the first act. All week long Ted continued to behave in the same manner that he had before. When we were warming up at a practice barre backstage he could not stop kissing my hands as they rested on the barre while I was exercising. There were no dancers around, just stagehands who were not paying attention. By now I certainly should have told him off, but I had an inability to do so. One evening I was walking back to the hotel after a performance when Ted caught up with me and we walked back together. We were alone when we got into the elevator. When it stopped at my floor, it occurred to me that I had the perfect opportunity to invite him to my room, but I had been so irritated with his behavior that I had lost my desire. From the expression on his face he looked as if he may have regretted the speech he made to me on the plane to Berlin. We both said good night, and I left him there and went alone to my room.

When we returned in the spring Balanchine choreographed a full-length production of *Coppelia* with Patricia McBride and Helgi Tomasson as the principal dancers. Because I was tall, I danced in the czardas. At the first rehearsal Balanchine suggested that the boys choose their partners and Francis asked me to dance with him. We had worked together before, and I enjoyed dancing with him. Lincoln Kirstein came to watch some of our rehearsals. He was the general director of the New York City Ballet and the president of SAB. Many years ago he had had a vision of an American ballet company and school. After seeing Balanchine's work in Europe, he made it possible for him to come to this country and fulfill that dream.

At the end of April we were scheduled to open the season with *Symphony in C*. We were onstage rehearsing the finale of the ballet with Balanchine for the opening night performance. I had just done a jump landing on my right foot when suddenly my ankle wobbled, my leg buckled under me, and I found myself on the floor. Balanchine happened to stop the rehearsal at this point in order to make a correction at the front of the stage. He did not see me immediately, but Rosemary did and came right over. A few dancers had gathered around me. I was unable to get up. Francis picked me up and carried me all the way to the elevator and up to the dressing room, where he put me down on the cot. While I was resting there, my foot began to swell, becoming increasingly painful. After a while Ned, who worked in the office, came in to offer to make an emergency doctor's appointment for me. When the rehearsal was over Rosemary came in to see how I was and I told her I had a doctor's appointment. I had worn boots to the theater and couldn't get the boot on my foot, so Donna gave me her clogs and she wore my boots. When I arrived at the doctor's office there were so many patients ahead of me that I had to wait two hours before he would see me. While I was waiting I became aware of a ball forming on the side of my foot, which became progressively larger, and by the time the doctor saw me even he was shocked. After X-rays and an examination he determined that I had a chip bone fracture. He bandaged the foot and gave me a prescription. I would not be dancing for a long time.

The next day my grandmother came to stay with me to help out with the shopping and cooking so that I could stay off my foot. About two weeks later my parents returned from Europe, and shortly after that Sally moved into her own apartment. While my foot was healing I debated whether to go back to the company or not. After having suffered several injuries I had to think very hard whether I wanted to continue in a profession that was so hazardous to my body. If I did not go back, it meant changing my career and retraining in another field. My whole life had been devoted to ballet and music. I was very ambitious and wanted to be a principal dancer with the company and eventually choreograph. I could not conceive of giving up and changing my life at this point despite the injuries.

After a month that included physical therapy at the doctor's office my foot healed and I was ready to start working out. I went to the theater to tell Rosemary that I would be coming back. They were rehearsing *A Midsummer Night's Dream*, and I sat down to watch. Afterward everyone was very friendly and wanted to know if I would be returning. Rosemary was pleased to be able to put my name down to start in Saratoga. It was the beginning of June and I had a month to get ready. I thought I would work at home in my bedroom, where I had enough space to do a complete barre and some center work. When I put on my leotard and tights I realized that it would be better not to put ballet slippers on and put on a pair of socks over my tights instead. After working this way for a few days, doing some basic exercises holding onto a chair, I progressed to ballet slippers and eventually to point shoes. When I did my first *relevé* on point I felt exhilarated with the progress I had made. At first I worked out once a day, gradually increasing the amount of hours by working twice a day in order to build stamina. My knee and hip injuries had healed with the month's rest, but soon after working out they became aggravated again, especially the left hip. This depressed me. I had hoped to go back without any injuries, and now I would have to go back with a hip problem. But I had made a commitment to dance, and I was not going to go back on my word.

I took the company bus to Saratoga and got my old room at the Rip Van Dam. Later in the day I went to the theater to reserve a place in the dressing room. As I was walking down the driveway I saw a familiar figure sitting just outside the stage door. It was Balanchine. We said hello and I explained to him what had happened to me. The next day I saw Ted at the theater. He gave me a big bear hug, welcoming me back, and seemed genuinely glad to see me. I didn't feel angry with him anymore. During the week Rosemary asked me to do a few performances of *Swan Lake* for a newer dancer who was injured. I had recently gotten out of the ballet. When newer dancers were put into the ballet, older dancers were taken out, and it had been my turn to get out of it. We rehearsed the ballet onstage with Balanchine. When I had danced in my old place he had never given me special attention, but now that I was in another location and was the senior swan in the group, he watched me.

About a week later I was standing in the parking area waiting for a bus to town with three other dancers who were new in the company. Balanchine came walking up the driveway, and when he saw us he came over to offer us a lift. We all trooped over to his car and then we paused, because we had to decide who would sit in the front seat. Since I was the dancer with whom he was most familiar, it seemed logical for me to sit there, and there was something in his manner toward me that made me feel comfortable doing it. I was so used to seeing Balanchine in the studio and onstage that seeing him doing something mundane such as driving a car seemed odd. After making some small talk on the way to town, he asked us where we wanted to be let off. I suggested that he let us out across the street from the Grand Union, and when we got out we all thanked him for the ride.

That summer I was destined to meet Balanchine on several occasions outside the theater. After Saratoga the company flew to Los Angeles. I had taken a room at the Montecito Hotel and had just gotten into the elevator with my luggage when Balanchine tried to squeeze on with his. It looked as if the door was going to close on his arm and hand, and I quickly said, "Watch your hand, Mr. B." (Mr. B was the name dancers used when addressing him.) He seemed a little disoriented but quickly recovered. When the elevator stopped at his floor I offered to help him with his luggage. He was very appreciative but insisted that he could manage.

I continued on up to find my room. I had a lovely view of the Hollywood Hills and a fully equipped kitchen.

After unpacking and making a grocery list, I went to the supermarket, which was a block away from the hotel. My cart was already filled with groceries when just as I was turning the corner I nearly collided with Balanchine, who was also pushing a cart. Of course we had to stop and we both laughed. Then he looked into my cart to see what I was buying, but I didn't have the nerve to look into his cart.

We were performing at the Greek Theater for a week. One evening after dancing *Serenade*, I was in the hall on my way out of the theater when Rosemary stopped me to say that my performance had been "very good." I was surprised and pleased. Apparently, she had been watching from out front in the audience. It was unusual for the ballet mistress to compliment a member of the corps de ballet. Usually she could be seen after performances in the dressing room giving corrections to dancers, so I was especially pleased.

After LA, we did a week of performances at Wolftrap, followed by a short break and then a week in Philadelphia in September. During the summer my hip condition deteriorated, and by the time we went to Philadelphia it had become so painful and weak that I limped when I walked. We were performing *A Midsummer Night's Dream*, which meant that I had to dance every night. Somehow I managed to get through it despite the severe aggravation. When we returned home we had some time off before the rehearsal period began in October, and I hoped that the rest would do it some good. However, by the time we started rehearsing I realized that I would have to see a doctor.

After X-rays and thorough examination, he analyzed it to be a weakened muscle in the joint area and made two suggestions. I could either work with a therapist who had machines that could strengthen it or work with a private coach who might be able to figure out whether there was something in the way that I was working that was exacerbating the condition. Since I didn't know anything about the machines, I chose to work with a private coach because I thought I could benefit more from this approach.

When I explained everything to Rosemary, she was very supportive and said that I would come back stronger. Later when I spoke to Betty Cage about the leave of absence she told me that Balanchine was going to keep me on the payroll until I was ready to come back. I thought it was generous of him. As a general rule he did not approve of private coaches and preferred that the dancers take class with him. It seemed that in my case I had his approval.

I asked Peter Nelson if he would be available to work with me. I hadn't studied with him privately since I was a student but had been taking his regular class during layoffs. For the next six weeks we worked together every day. We analyzed and dissected every exercise at the barre, and in the center we concentrated on exercises that improved my balance and control. Through Peter's approach and method of working I was able to strengthen my hip and learned how to work with less strain on the joint. When I went back to the company I was better prepared for Balanchine's class and found that I enjoyed taking it for the first time. I was also better prepared for performances because Peter and I had worked out a series of exercises at the barre that catered to my particular needs.

I rejoined the company during the *Nutcracker*, and in January we resumed our regular repertory. I think Balanchine noticed the change in my work because when I took my place onstage to rehearse "Emeralds" with him, he watched me as I did the beginning movements of the ballet. At one point I had to pose on my knee at the front of the stage and then *bourrée* to stage left. When I did the *bourrée* he turned his head sharply to watch me do it. In the finale I was the first girl to enter from upstage left opposite another dancer. He focused on me as I did these movements. When I ran diagonally downstage and did a *développé* I felt that he was watching to see how high my extension was.

As the season progressed he continued to observe me in other rehearsals. There was one incident in class when I was standing at the barre with my supporting leg on point and the other leg raised to the side. I could see in the mirror that Balanchine was standing behind me, looking at me. I tried to raise my leg a little higher before bringing it down. On another occasion I was assisting Rosemary in teaching *Swan Lake* to some new members. We were in the main hall when Balanchine came in from the rear door, passing through to the front entrance where I was standing nearby. He smiled and bowed his head in recognition.

During one of the previous seasons Balanchine had made a speech after class asking the girls to try to cut back on the number of point shoes they were using because of the enormous expense. Roland Vasquez, a former dancer with the company, was in charge of ordering and distributing the shoes. Each week of the season we were permitted to have a certain amount of shoes with ribbon, and even after Balanchine's speech I always felt adequately supplied. Some of the dancers wore Freeds, and others wore Capezios. Because the Capezio was a lighter shade of pink, Balanchine asked the dancers who wore them to dye their shoes so that there would be one uniform color on stage. It took me a long time to figure out what shoes would be best for my needs. I found that I was most comfortable wearing Capezios with a half-shank. The half-shank made the shoe softer and more flexible. When I was a student, Danilova suggested that I wear something between the first two toes. I was not standing straight enough on point and had a tendency to lean toward the big toe because of a bunion. She said she had the same problem. From then on I wore a Dr. Scholls toe flex on each foot between the first and second toes and found that I felt better dancing with them.

During my time with the company new dancers were taken in every season and we expanded to almost one hundred dancers. When the company performed at City Center, it was smaller. With the move to Lincoln Center where we had a larger stage, Balanchine was able to make productions on a grander scale. The performing seasons lengthened and subscription series became popular. The school became world-renowned, turning out highly trained dancers, and the company reached the pinnacle of its success as one of the greatest companies in the world.

In January, Suzanne Farrell returned after a six-year absence. I remembered seeing her perform many times when I was a student during the 1960s and was inspired by her. She was given her old roles back, but some of them she had to share with other dancers who had been dancing them in her absence.

This season I was dancing a great deal. In *Jewels* I was in "Emeralds" and "Diamonds," and in *Symphony in C* I did both the first and third movements of the ballet. I finally graduated from a monster to a princess in *Firebird*, and I was given the role of one of the sisters in *Prodigal Son*. There was no dancing, just pantomime, but it was a conspicuous part because there are only three women in the ballet. I appeared at the beginning and the end when the Prodigal Son returns home. I also performed *La Source* and *La Valse* and learned *Agon* and *Movements for Piano and Orchestra*. These two ballets were not easy to learn, because Stravinsky's music is atonal. Because of the lack of traditional melody, it is very difficult to count. By this time I had performed over thirty ballets in the repertory. Although my hip was not completely healed, it was my best season because of the improvements that I had made with Peter's help and because Balanchine was beginning to show a real interest in my work.

The season ended in February with *Don Quixote*, and I danced in the first act in the new section that Balanchine had added. We wore brilliant red tutus, and I really enjoyed these performances. I did not realize then that these would be my last performances.

Chapter 10
Rehabilitation

Balanchine was planning a Ravel Festival for the spring season of 1975, and we only had two weeks off before we were called back to begin rehearsals. I was scheduled to work with John Taras, who was choreographing *Daphnis and Chloe*. Our rehearsals were held at one of the studios at SAB in the Juilliard building. On the second day I felt a pull on the inside of my left foot and some pain afterward. At first I thought it was only a foot strain and continued to work on it for two more weeks wearing ballet slippers instead of point shoes. When the pain did not go away I went to the doctor to have it checked out. To my horror, the diagnosis was sprained ligaments on the inside of my foot. I couldn't believe it. I was out again with another major injury. I was so angry and frustrated that for the first time I wanted to stop dancing. My family thought I should ask for an extended leave of absence in case I changed my mind later on, and after I calmed down I agreed that that was the best thing to do.

I went to the theater to talk to Balanchine and waited for him in the hallway on the fifth floor near the back entrance where he usually came in for class. A few minutes after eleven o'clock in the morning the elevator door opened and Balanchine emerged. I explained what had happened and asked for the leave. My face must have shown all the agony and frustration that I felt. He nodded, saying "yes" to the leave, taking it all in his stride. He was used to the dancers' problems. His own career had ended with a knee injury.

Later, I told Rosemary and went to get my things out of my theater case. I decided to keep my locker on the fifth floor, because I wasn't sure if I was coming back.

This injury was different than the chip bone fracture I had the year before because it took much longer to heal. I had been an avid reader while in the company, and as I sat there with my foot up, soaking it in Epsom salts every few hours, I read every single book we had in the apartment. When therapy was started my foot became more painful, increasing my dependency on the medication. Since it would have been unhealthy to remain on high dosages of the drug, therapy was discontinued. Subsequently I was able to reduce the medication and slowly progressed to walking. However, I was left with muscle damage in both feet.

During the summer I began working out. I could do the barre and some center work, but my feet were not strong enough to wear point shoes. My back, which had troubled me on and off, became worse. I experienced pain in the upper back and weakness in my arms. I noticed this when playing the piano and going about daily activities. During this time I listened to the music of my ballet and made changes based on what I had learned working with friends in the company. When the fall season started I thought I would go to the theater to ask Violette Verdy for advice about my foot injury and I wanted to ask Balanchine if I could work with the students at the school on my ballet. During a matinee performance I was lucky to find Violette backstage warming up at the practice barre. She greeted me warmly, and we arranged to talk in her dressing room after the performance. Balanchine was there also and he greeted me cordially, shaking my hand. I told him I was getting better and asked him if I could work with the students on my ballet. He hesitated for a moment and then nodded in approval. His approval was all that I needed to feel inspired to go ahead with the project. Meanwhile Violette advised me to go to a therapist who had machines that would build muscle in my feet, making it possible to dance. She warned me that the woman was a difficult person and could be unpleasant to work with. But Violette felt that the results I would get with the machines would make it worthwhile.

I was so eager to get started on my project that I postponed going to the therapist and went to the school. I spoke to Miss Gleboff, an administrative director who had been there when I was a student, and explained that Balanchine had given me permission to work with the students. I was allowed to use students in the advanced and professional divisions and planned to observe classes so that I could decide whom I would be using and what roles they would be dancing. Doubrovska and Danilova were still teaching and were glad to see me.

In order to select the boys I had to watch the boys' class, which was taught by Stanley Williams. Rudolf Nureyev happened to be taking the class when I walked in to observe. He was standing at the barre facing the mirror, and the only chair in the room was a few feet in front of him. I had taken off my coat and put it on my lap, but it must have been blocking his view, because he gestured to me to move it so that he could see his foot in the mirror.

I wasn't sure which boys were available to use, so afterward I went to see Miss Gleboff again to get a list. Madame Tumkovsky happened to be in her office and was very helpful in giving me the information and seemed enthusiastic about my project. It was important to watch the adagio class to see how the boys and girls danced together and to see what the boys' abilities were in partnering. Richard Rapp, a former soloist with the company, taught the class. I was pleased to see that he assigned two girls to each boy so that everyone had a partner and no one was left out. After ten days I made a final decision on the dancers that I was going to use. I was just getting ready to put a notice on the bulletin board calling my first rehearsal when Miss Gleboff came up to me to say Balanchine was canceling the project because it would interfere with the coming workshop rehearsals. She also said that Nolan T'Sani, who had wanted to do a ballet, had his project canceled as well. I was deeply upset, but I didn't think I could talk to Balanchine about it. I saw no alternative but to make an appointment with the therapist.

The machines were remarkable, but the therapist was more than difficult. She screamed at me throughout the entire session even though I was perfectly willing to do everything that she asked of me. She drove me from one exercise to the next without stopping, and when it was over I collapsed onto a lounge chair, totally exhausted, as she bullied me into signing up for ten sessions payable in advance. I could feel the improvement in my feet immediately, and although I knew what I was up against, I felt at her mercy. I gave her a check for $100, and for the next ten days I worked in a continuous state of exhaustion. The weather turned bitterly cold, with the mercury hovering around zero degrees for several days in a row.

After completing the first ten sessions I became ill in a way that I had never experienced before. I didn't have a cold or fever but was totally weakened and bedridden for a while.

When I recovered I went back and completed a second

set of sessions. After I signed up for a third set I became ill again and decided not to go back. When I talked to the therapist on the phone and asked for a refund, she was unpleasant about it. I wasn't sure if she was going to give me my money back. A few days later I received my check in the mail with a note saying: "Feel better soon."

Around this time I received a notice from the Workmen's Compensation Board stating that a hearing was to be held at the World Trade Center regarding my chip bone fracture and current injury. I hadn't received any compensation from them or the company, and my case was now due. When I went to the hearing the judge advised me to get a lawyer to represent me and set a date for another hearing. I was also scheduled to be examined by a doctor provided by the Compensation Board. While I was there I met Deni Lamont, a soloist with the company, who was also waiting for a hearing. He recommended that I go to Pilates for my injury, where they had the same machines as the other therapist, but the atmosphere was more relaxed. My father found a lawyer who was experienced in this type of case, and when I returned for the second hearing I was awarded $2,500.

In the spring I went to Pilates, where I was able to work at my own pace. In addition to muscle therapy, I worked at home every day doing exercises at the barre and center work. Despite all of the therapy I had undergone, I still could not dance on point.

On the Memorial Day weekend I was home alone in the apartment and was talking to my grandmother on the phone when I felt a terrible pain in my left arm and shoulder. After I got off the phone I could feel a huge spasm in the upper left side of my back. In addition to the pain I felt a weakening of both arms. I used a heating pad for my back, as I was accustomed to doing whenever my back had bothered me before. At this time my parents and I were in the process of moving to a smaller apartment in Lincoln Towers, which was a complex of buildings near Lincoln Center. With the busyness of moving I postponed going to the doctor and continued to use a heating pad, thinking that the condition would go away. When I realized that it wasn't going away, I finally went to the doctor. Instead of going back to the one who had treated me for my previous injuries, I went to a new doctor highly recommended by a family friend. He diagnosed the problem as muscle weakness, and I began working with his therapist. I was given exercises to do that involved trying to raise myself on my arms and hands while lying on my stomach and another one standing that involved leaning with my hands on the wall and pushing with my arms as if I were doing push-ups on the wall. These exercises aggravated me more than they helped. The therapist happened to leave at this time, and I worked with a new therapist who give me a balletic exercise that concentrated on movement of the arm joints. This also failed.

After three months of therapy and very little progress I went to see my father's doctor. He recommended a therapist who he said was the best.

We made an appointment and because of my condition, my father had to accompany me. I couldn't handle any weight and had great difficulty getting in and out of my coat. I couldn't use a bus or subway. I could only travel by cab or private car, and I couldn't open a car door or any heavy door to get into a building. When we arrived, a young woman showed me into a room and told me to take my slacks and sweater off, after which she assisted me onto a table with a mattress, where I lay down under a sheet. Because the weather was cold I had worn snuggies under my slacks and decided to keep these on. I had always stayed in my clothes to exercise with the other therapists. A few minutes later a very tall man, over six feet, came into the room wearing a suit and tie. He appeared to be about fifty years old. His manner was friendly and he introduced himself, saying that he had spoken to my doctor and knew a little bit about my background. He went out of the room and returned shortly after wearing a white smock. The first thing he did was pull my arm back. It hurt terribly and would not go all the way back. Then he said that I should not carry anything and should shift my position every twenty minutes. I felt that he understood my condition completely. I had already discovered that I couldn't stay in one position very long because of the pain and weakness and I certainly couldn't carry anything. After this he assisted me off the table so he could see how I walked. When I got back on the table he pushed my right knee several times to my chest while I was lying on my back and we repeated the exercise with the left leg. Then he pushed both knees to my chest at the same time. I was to do these exercises twice a day and report back to him the following week.

After I got dressed I felt remarkably better and a little more optimistic. I didn't realize then that this was the beginning of a ten-year association in which the therapist would become a real friend through the ups and downs of my condition.

Unfortunately, my body did not respond as well to the exercises at home, and when I returned I made my complaints. The therapist gave me a heat treatment and a massage of my back and chest muscles. Then he stretched my arms back one at a time. This was very painful, but he knew exactly how much pressure to apply so as not to injure me. After this my response to the exercises was better and I continued the treatments once a week.

The therapist suggested that I see Dr. Hamilton, who,

coincidentally, was the doctor for the New York City Ballet. I hadn't gone to him before because he was new at the time that I was there and I had my own doctor. After examining me, he could not determine the cause of the muscle weakness and sent me to a neurologist associated with the Roosevelt Hospital. This doctor thought I might have the beginning stages of muscular dystrophy, but he was not sure and sent me to a neurologist at the New York Hospital. I was given tests for muscle disease. The results were negative and the official diagnosis was severe muscle weakness, with intensive physical therapy recommended. The doctor gave me the name of a therapist, but I preferred to stay with mine.

I still had insurance coverage from the company, which would pay 80 percent of my therapy bills before it expired in three months. I asked my therapist if he would work with me every day, and we began an intensive program. We started each session with heat, massage, and stretching. I did a series of resistance exercises in various positions, pressing my arms against his to strengthen and build muscle. We also exercised the legs, which strengthened the back at the same time. When I got off the table I felt better and in less pain.

In spite of the progress I was making, I remained deeply depressed. It was not just the loss of my career and that I would never dance again; what was troubling me more was the realization that I had a crippling disability and would not be able to lead a normal life. This was hard to face, and I gave in to crying and wallowing in self-pity. My parents thought I ought to see a psychiatrist for my depression. At first my response was negative, because I didn't think that talking about it would help, but I agreed to try it for a while and went to a doctor whose office was across the street in one of the other buildings in Lincoln Towers. He gave me antidepressant medication that made me feel more peaceful and did help to ease some of the despair and hopelessness that I felt. After about three months, I was better and withdrew gradually from the medication. I also stopped seeing the psychiatrist.

Around this time Sally ran into a company member who recommended another doctor. I went to see him with the hope that he might have something new to offer. He said that the therapy I was doing was not intensive enough and suggested that I use a pulley-and-weight machine at home as well. He arranged for me to go to the Burke Rehabilitation Hospital, where I would learn to use the machine and receive an intensive therapy program.

My parents and I made the trip to White Plains, where the hospital, surrounded by green lawns and flowering shrubbery, was located. The facilities were very impressive. I was put into the orthopedic ward, where most of the amputee patients were. My roommate had one leg missing, and after introducing myself I explained what was wrong with me.

I arrived on a Friday and was wheeled down to occupational therapy in the afternoon. After the session it was decided that I didn't need the wheelchair because I was ambulatory and could walk to all my programs. Most of the patients used wheelchairs.

Meals were served in our rooms, and each patient had his own table on wheels. We used plastic utensils and Styrofoam paper cups, and I found that I was more comfortable with the lightweight tableware.

I was accustomed to taking a shower every evening before bedtime. A shower was effective in easing my pain, and it stimulated the muscles. The shower room, which was down the hall, was designed to make it easier for patients and nurses. The dial to regulate the water temperature was on the exterior wall of the shower so the nurse could regulate it. There was a bench next to the stall shower and a signal button one could press if one needed help.

On the weekend I was upset because there was no therapy. I had expected to exercise right away. Therapy was given every day during the week, and on weekends patients rested and had visitors. My family came to see me every weekend.

On Monday I was given a card with my schedule of classes. I started my day with mat class. The therapist worked with me individually. We did a series of exercises designed to strengthen my arms and back and to make my back more flexible. The mat was low on legs, making it easy for patients to get on and off. After my session there was a short time to rest, and then I went downstairs to hydrotherapy. There was a large swimming pool heated at 100 degrees. Patients who could not get into the pool on their own were lifted in a chair. I had always been a good swimmer, but now it was difficult to raise my arms to swim. I had to be content with floating and moving around in the water. After lunch I was scheduled for occupational therapy, where we concentrated on strengthening the arms and hands. I worked with clay and to improve my mobility I played a game of catch outside with the therapist using a lightweight ball. I also played Ping-Pong. I may have been disabled, but I played a great game of Ping-Pong as long as I didn't have to pick up the ball when it dropped on the floor. This was awkward for me. My last class was gym. Here amputee patients learned to walk with a false leg. I used the pulley-and-weight machine, which strengthened my back and arms, and I used another machine which strengthened the legs.

I spent one month at the hospital. When I came home, I still had muscle weakness, but I was stronger and able to do more. I was also more confident and better able to cope with my problem and live with it.

Chapter 11
A New Direction

The first thing I did when I came home from the hospital was buy a pulley-and-weight machine. Dad put up a metal bar in the door frame of the closet. Attached to it were two ropes with handles and bags into which different sized weights could be put.

About six months later I replaced this with a professional machine such as I had used at Burke, which was installed on my bedroom wall. I used the machine every day and went to my physical therapist three times a week.

Now that I was better I wanted to find an interest that would take me out of the house and get my mind off my condition. I thought of taking singing lessons with a teacher who had known my father for many years. I had a good voice and enjoyed singing, often accompanying myself on the piano. When I was at SAB I studied for a short period of time with a teacher who thought I had potential, but I gave up the lessons because I wanted to dance. At this time I did not entertain the idea of a career in singing; I just wanted to be involved with music and thought that standing and vocalizing would be good for my posture, strengthening for my muscles, and build stamina. I studied several months with the teacher.

During this time Donna, who had left the company before I did, came to visit bringing with her a shopping bag full of books. She was going to a university in New York, taking courses in a special program. This program was for students over twenty-one years of age and offered a total of forty credits in a variety of courses toward a college degree. Donna encouraged me to go and I thought about it a great deal while reading her books. I wanted to meet new people and learn new things, but I had some anxiety about whether I could get around the building with my disability. Students were required to have a high school diploma and pass an entry exam to be eligible. I had my diploma, but it had been a long time since I had taken a test. There were several dates scheduled for the exam, and finally, on the last available date, my father drove my mother and me to the school, where she helped me find the examination room. Everyone was sitting at tables, and she assisted in seating me at one of them. It was December and I had worn a heavy coat, which I couldn't handle, so she took it home with her and arranged to come back in three hours when the exam would be over.

The exam was not easy. There were three parts. I thought I did well in the vocabulary section and writing an essay, but I wasn't sure about the reading comprehension. I didn't like to read under pressure and answer questions in a hurry. When the exam was over I had to ask the person next to me to pull my chair out because I couldn't push it back to get up. I had overcome my first hurdle. If I was going to go to school, it meant that I would have to ask for help occasionally without being self-conscious or embarrassed.

About two weeks later I received a letter from the school stating that I had passed the exam and was accepted. My family and I celebrated my success, and shortly afterward I registered for my first course. I chose World Issues, which met once a week for three hours. The course was stimulating, and the teacher was handsome. The class was small, and I enjoyed the discussions we had. The issues turned out to be capitalism, imperialism, racism, and sexism. In the middle of the course the teacher encouraged the students to volunteer to make speeches about subjects they had personal knowledge of that were relevant to the issues. I thought that my tour of Russia and Poland with the company would be interesting for the class. Two of the books we were reading, *The Twilight of Capitalism* and *A Critique of American Foreign Policy in the Cold War*, had a pro-Russian viewpoint. I suspected that the teacher may have had leanings in that direction. Privately it amused me to think that after he heard about the drain stopper, toilet paper, and food, as well as some other things, he might feel differently. I let the teacher know when I was ready to give my speech, and he invited me to sit at his desk in front of the class while he took a seat at one of the desks. It was like being onstage again, and I wasn't nervous at all. Afterward the students and teacher asked me questions. In retrospect, the title of one of those books should have been *The Twilight of Communism*.

In the summer I took another course, called Culture and Society. Since courses were expensive, I applied for a TAP grant and was awarded financial aid for the summer and fall semesters. President Carter was generous in helping college students. In the fall I took literature, science, and opera appreciation. When I was at PCS I had taken one year of general science and substituted a second foreign language for biology and physics. Now I had the opportunity to catch up on all the science that I had missed, and I found that I really liked it. The more I learned, the more I wanted to know. Opera appreciation was especially enjoyable. The teacher was familiar with the Patelson Music House. During the semester he asked us to see some performances of the opera. The City Opera was having its usual season at the State Theater before the New York City Ballet began its season, and I went to see Mozart's *Marriage of Figaro*, Puccini's *La Bohème*, and Bizet's *Carmen*. They were wonderful productions, and afterward Dad bought the records so I could vocalize again.

While I was going to school I continued to go to therapy regularly. One morning I was in the lobby of the building where my therapist had his office. I was waiting for my father to pick me up with the car when, to my surprise, Balanchine walked into the lobby. As soon as he saw me he recognized me. We said hello and I gave him a kiss on the cheek. He was going to see a doctor in the building. I told him that I had to stop dancing because of my injuries, but I didn't have the heart to tell him I was disabled. It made me very happy to see him again.

For the next semester I applied to OVR (Vocational Rehabilitation) for financial aid. I had to submit papers from two doctors confirming my disability and was assigned a counselor to keep track of my progress. The TAP grant required that one take a certain amount of credits, but with OVR I had the freedom to work more slowly at my own pace. This semester I took history and another course in science.

On my first class in science the professor gave a lecture. He appeared to be in his mid-thirties and had a beard all over his face. At the end of the session he handed out homework questions.

On the following week we were going over some of the homework in class before handing it in and the professor happened to be standing near my desk. When one of the students was reading her answer, his eye caught mine and he smiled, so I returned the smile.

On the third class I was sitting in the front row when

the professor came in. He gazed at me in such a way that it dawned on me that he was interested. After about an hour and a half, he gave a fifteen-minute break. Everyone left the room except another student, the professor, and myself. The three of us talked mainly about science. If there had been just the two of us, we might have talked of other things.

When I went home I couldn't get my mind off him and looked forward with great anticipation to the next class. This time when he came in he had shaved his beard and I really saw what he looked like. He was an attractive and virile-looking man. During the class, we had our first test. I finished a little sooner than the others and brought my paper over to him where he was standing by the window. He said, "You look like a dancer." He had guessed my profession. I told him that I had to stop dancing because of an injury, but I didn't say anything about my disability. I wasn't sure if he had noticed that someone usually helped me with my coat and the door. After I went back to my seat, I decided to hand in my homework. He had gone back to his desk, and I went up to him. At the beginning of the semester he had written his name on the blackboard. It was a difficult Irish name. I asked him if this was the correct way of saying his name and pronounced it for him. He said it was correct and added in a low, sexy voice, "You get an A for the course." I went back to my desk knowing now why he had shaved his beard.

As the course progressed there were occasional opportunities to talk, and toward the end of the semester he invited the class to go to the Hayden Planetarium. Actually, we were invited by another teacher to join his class on Sunday. I hadn't been there since I was a little girl and was eager to see it again. My father drove me over, and when I arrived everyone was waiting outside. I was surprised to see that no one from my class had shown up except one student and the professor. This student was a friendly young woman who was aware of my condition and had helped me in class. It was a beautiful spring day. We chatted for a while and then followed the other class inside. We went upstairs to the auditorium, and when we entered it was pitch-dark. I suddenly felt off balance and insecure. I said the professor's name with some anxiety in my voice. He was right behind me and took my hand to steady me. A minute or so later the lights went on and we found seats a few rows away from the other class. As we were about to sit down I saw that the seat was up. The other young woman quickly pushed it down as he took my coat off and we all sat down. After the show, she told us she was joining her husband and children next door at the Museum of Natural History and we two were left alone. It was fate bringing us together. He went over to the other teacher to thank him, and by the time we were downstairs in the lobby we had decided to go to the museum and have lunch. There was a woman sitting at a table who had buttons that one could attach to one's clothing. This enabled one to get into the museum without charge. As he attached the button to my collar it must have been evident to the woman who was observing us that we were extremely attracted to each other.

My father was supposed to pick me up with the car, but when we got outside he was nowhere to be seen. Instead there was a long line of cars blocking the driveway waiting to get a parking space for the next show. As we started walking up the block I saw a phone booth on the corner and thought I should call Mother to tell her what my plans were, but just then a car honked. It was my father, who had turned onto the street from Central Park West, and I waved him on.

Once the professor and I were in the museum I remembered it very well. He had also been here before. I tired very easily and after a short while we decided to have lunch. There was a cafeteria downstairs where we had to wait on line. When I saw that I had to slide a tray as well as carry it to a table I knew that I was incapable of doing this without hurting myself. I might even drop it. I felt impelled to tell him what was wrong with me. He suggested that I sit down and he would get the lunch for both of us. It was so crowded that the only available space was next to an elderly couple. When he joined me with our lunch we had our first really long conversation, completely oblivious to the noise and people around us.

After lunch we walked down Central Park West heading in the direction of my apartment. We were going to take a cab, but there were none to be found. By the time we got to Seventy-second Street I was exhausted. A cab came along and even though we were a short distance from my home, we took it. I asked the professor if he would like to come up and meet my parents. He said he would and he ended up staying for an hour. It was a happy ending to a fulfilling day.

I had been thinking for some time about going to see a performance of the ballet and thought I might be able to get viewing-room seats. The viewing room was in the back of the orchestra, where seats were reserved for dancers' friends, relatives, the press, and other guests. It occurred to me that my new friend might enjoy seeing the ballet, and on the next class I went over to him during the break and asked him. He was very enthusiastic and offered to get the tickets. I explained that I could get viewing-room seats, which were free. After class we exchanged phone numbers.

During the week I called the theater and spoke to a secretary about the tickets, but she wouldn't give them to me. I wasn't going to give up so easily and called Edward

Bigelow, who was the assistant manager of the company. He was very cordial and gave me two tickets for May 23. When I went back to school for the final exam I wrote the date of the performance on a piece of paper and attached it to my exam. When I gave it to the professor he said he would call me. A few days later he did to say that I had passed the course and he had given me an A. After this good news he suggested that we have dinner on the same evening as the ballet.

After dining at Fiorello's, a popular Italian restaurant across the street from the theater, we walked over to pick up our tickets at the box office. When I asked for them, they weren't there. Eddie had goofed. He must have forgotten to arrange them after he talked to me on the phone. Tom Kelley, the manager of the theater, was in the lobby, and I told him what had happened. He saved the evening by giving us two red velvet chairs, which were placed alongside the fifth row of the orchestra. We were much closer to the stage than we would have been if we had sat in the viewing room.

The first ballet on the program was *Interplay*, with choreography by Robbins. It was the first time I had come to see a performance since I left. As the curtain rose I felt an immediate sense of recognition, of myself onstage, the excitement that comes with the first sounds of the music; then, turning to look at my companion, I felt content to be where I was, in the audience with a sense of pride to have been a member of the company. The next ballet was *La Source*, with Merrill Ashley and Peter Martins as the leading dancers. The company looked good, and it was a pleasure to watch both Robbins and Balanchine ballets.

On the second intermission we tried to go backstage, but the usher would not let us pass. Just then a former dancer with the company who worked in the office came out and told the usher that it was okay. Hugo Fiorato, who was conducting this evening's performance, greeted me with a big hug, and I introduced him to my friend. As we went around the corner to a larger area, we ran into Peter Martins, who shook my hand, wanting to know how I was. Peter, who had been a principal with the Royal Danish Ballet, had joined the company in 1969 and soon Balanchine would be grooming him to take his place.

Nothing had changed. Backstage looked the same with the practice barre, resin box, and pail of water that was there for the girls to dunk their heels to keep their point shoes from slipping off. A few dancers who worked with me stopped to say hello. Renee Estopinal commented that there were so many new dancers that she did not know who they were. Patricia McBride, who was warming up at the practice barre, asked me how long it had been since I had left. She couldn't believe that it had been four years. The professor was interested in examining the lights that were on the floor and above in the wings while I took a few steps and stood onstage. At this moment I felt nostalgic, remembering the exhilaration of being onstage. When intermission was over we returned to our seats for the last ballet, which was *Union Jack*. Balanchine had choreographed this ballet for the bicentennial a year after I left the company. It was a wonderful, witty, and spirited extravaganza. My friend enjoyed the evening very much, and I learned that he had seen the company before. Perhaps he had seen me dance.

We saw each other one more time before he went away for the summer. While he was away I spent time socializing with friends of Sally and mine. I was feeling good about myself and was doing the best I could with my disability. I was happy at school and with the new man in my life. I continued to go to therapy three times a week. My therapist had always been interested in knowing more about the technique of ballet and specifically what the exercises were. I offered to give him and his assistant a ballet class. On a day when I was not having my own therapy, I came in on their lunch hour. The therapist and his assistant used one of the tables as a barre, and I was able to demonstrate the exercises for them. I explained how they should stand, and we began the *pliés*. We went through the barre work and they did amazingly well for two people who did not know anything about ballet. It was a lot of fun and afterward we all went out to lunch. I had a daiquiri, which I drank with a straw.

In the fall I returned to school to take a course in mathematics and the Life Achievement Program. Math had never been my best subject, but the woman who taught the course made it easy to understand. The Life Achievement Program was designed to give students credit towards a college degree if they could demonstrate knowledge and experience in their own field. I discussed in depth the intensive training in ballet and my working experiences, travels, injuries, and subsequent rehabilitation. I stated that in addition to performing, I was qualified to teach and stage ballets. Students in this program were required to give documented proof. Miss Gleboff gave me a letter stating that I had completed the beginners, intermediate, advanced, and professional divisions at SAB from 1964 to 1970. Betty Cage also gave me a letter confirming my years with the company from 1970 to 1975. The report was judged by a panel of faculty members, and students could earn up to thirty credits. When I handed in my report, I stopped by the professor's office to give him a copy. We had renewed our friendship in the fall, and I thought it would be interesting for him to know more about ballet and what my life was like before he knew me.

A couple of weeks later I invited him to dinner at the apartment. Because it was difficult for me to cook, my mother and I decided that it would be best to serve cold cuts. I asked Mother to get a couple of albums out of the closet to put on the coffee table. One album had pictures of my trips, and the other contained old programs and mementos that I had saved over the years. My parents went out for the evening, giving us the privacy of the apartment.

When the professor arrived I asked him what he thought of the report. He said, "It was great." He also said that he had tried to put his feet in fifth position after reading the description of the positions of the feet.

We sat down on the couch to look at the albums. I hadn't looked at them for a long time. I still had my Kremlin pass with my name in Russian and some pins that I had bought from children on the street. There were old programs of the company and the Ballets de San Juan. I also had a photograph of myself dancing in Napoli in the workshop. I had saved newspaper articles of the Stravinsky Festival and articles that were written about the company while we were performing in Russia and Poland.

My father was painting a portrait of me, and it stood on his easel in the living room. The last season I was in the company we had been photographed for a New York City Ballet book and he was making a painting from the photograph. My friend took some time to examine this. Then we sat down to dinner. The apartment was on the twenty-sixth floor. The dining room was by the windows, and across the way the twinkling lights from the buildings overlooking the gardens below made a cozy and romantic atmosphere. I had known the professor for nine months. I had guessed right about his age. He was thirty-five and was eight years older than myself. I felt that he was a mature and sensitive man. While we were dining and talking, an overwhelming feeling came over me. I really thought he was the right person for me, and this evening turned out to be the beginning of a love affair that was to last for many years to come.

Epilogue

Balanchine, with his phenomenal creativity, has made the greatest contribution to the world of dance in the twentieth century. Going beyond the classic story ballet, he envisioned dance movement to music with one being an integral part of the other. A prime example is *Concerto Barocco* for two violins and string orchestra. Here he used his dancers to represent the instruments of the orchestra, fully realizing Bach's music in dance. Balanchine's style had developed through the years since his departure from Russia and during his association with Diaghilev's Ballet Russe de Monte Carlo. His *Apollo* in 1928, with music by Stravinsky, was innovative and a milestone in the conceptual approach to ballet. This work was the first of the *Greek Trilogy*, followed by *Orpheus* in 1948 and *Agon* in 1957, revealing his developing neoclassicism. In the intervening years and up until his death, he has choreographed over one hundred ballets. Illustrative of his innovative approach, contrary to the classic turned-out position, he would have his dancers turn in their feet and bodies in angular positions. This was inspired by the modern idiom of the contemporary music of Stravinsky, Hindemith, Webern, and others. All of Balanchine's ballets express the mood of the music, unfolding a panorama of human emotions, of love, tenderness, joy, sadness, regret, exuberance, and with it all his wit and sense of fun. Balanchine did not consider himself an originator. The classic ballet was his bible. His genius was in his brilliant style. He was a showman and his purpose was to entertain. The range of his work spanned from the baroque style of Bach to the jazz-influenced pop of Gershwin.

Working with Balanchine and the New York City Ballet demanded total involvement physically and emotionally. The pressures were enormous. It was extraordinary and rewarding to be there with him, as he, in his quiet way, moved us and the audience to the beauty of music.

Glossary

Positions of the Feet

FIRST POSITION. Heels together, feet turned out in a straight line.

SECOND POSITION. Feet turned out in a straight line separated by the distance of one foot.

THIRD POSITION. Feet turned out with heel of one foot in front of the middle of the other foot.

FOURTH POSITION. Feet turned out with one foot in front of the other, separated by the distance of one foot. Toes and heels are in line with each other.

FIFTH POSITION. Feet turned out with the right heel in front of the joint of the left big toe and vice versa.

Positions of the Arms (according to Cecchetti)

FIRST POSITION. Arms are held down and curved, the fingers almost touching the thighs.

SECOND POSITION. Arms are extended to the side.

THIRD POSITION. One arm is held down and curved in front of the body, and the other is extended low to the side.

FOURTH POSITION. One arm is extended to the side, and the other arm is curved either above the head or in front of the body on a level with the diaphragm.

FIFTH POSITION. Arms are curved down in front of the body or on a level with the diaphragm or above the head.

Exercises at the Barre

DEMI-PLIÉ. Bend the knees over the toes, keeping the heels down. Legs are turned out from the hips down.

GRAND PLIÉ. Deep knee bend, allowing the heels to come up. Legs are turned out from the hips down.

PORT DE BRAS. Bend forward and backward from the waist, coordinating the arm in a flowing and continuous movement.

BATTEMENT TENDU. Slide and point foot on the floor. Can be done to the front, side, and back.

BATTEMENT DÉGAGÉ. Slide and point foot off the floor two or three inches. Can be done to the front, side, and back.

BATTEMENT FRAPPÉ. Place pointed foot on front of ankle (working knee is bent and turned out) and extend leg, brushing foot low off the floor. Return foot to front or back of ankle. Can be done to the front, side, and back.

PETITS BATTEMENTS SUR LE COU DE PIED. Place pointed foot on front of ankle (working knee is bent and turned out); then move foot to back of ankle. Repetitive movement front to back, holding knee in place.

BATTEMENTS BATTUS. A series of beats with pointed foot on the front of the ankle. (Working knee is bent and turned out.)

ROND DE JAMBE À TERRE. Semicircle with foot pointed on the floor, lowering heel as it passes through first position.

ROND DE JAMBE EN L'AIR. Slide foot and extend leg to the side (forty-five degrees). Make circles with lower part of leg, holding knee in place.

RETIRÉ (PASSER). Raise pointed foot below the knee of supporting leg. (Working knee is bent and turned out.)

BATTEMENT FONDU. *Demi-plié* on supporting leg while bending working leg, pointing foot in front of ankle.

Straighten supporting leg simultaneously extending and straightening working leg (forty-five degrees). Can be done to the front, side, and back.

BATTEMENT DÉVELOPPÉ. Raise pointed foot on the front of supporting ankle. (Working knee is bent and turned out.) Raise foot higher on supporting leg and then extend leg outward (ninety degrees), gradually straightening knee. Can be done to the front, side, and back.

GRAND ROND DE JAMB EN L' AIR. *Développé* to the front and move the leg to the side and to the back in one continuous movement.

GRAND BATTEMENT. Slide foot and extend leg off the floor (ninety degrees or higher) with straight knee. Can be done to the front, side, and back.

RELEVÉ. Raise the heel and stand on the ball of the foot or on point. Can be done on two feet or one. It is often preceded by *demi-plié*.

ÉCHAPPÉ. From fifth position *demi-plié*, spring into second position onto the balls of the feet or on point.

SOUSSOUS. From fifth position *demi-plié*, spring into fifth position onto the balls of the feet or on point.

Center

ÉPAULEMENT. Directions of the body. Head, arms, and legs are coordinated in various positions (*croisé, éffacé, écarté, en face*).

PORT DE BRAS. Flowing and continuous movement of the arms in various positions.

TEMPS LIÉ. A combination of leg and arm movements based on three positions of the feet: fourth, fifth, and second.

ATTITUDE EN AVANT. Extension of the leg to the front with the knee bent.

ATTITUDE EN ARRIÉRE. Extension of the leg to the back with the knee bent.

ARABESQUE. Straight extension of the leg to the back.

RENVERSE. A movement that includes *grand rond de jambe en l'air* with *relevé* on supporting leg, ending with a *pas de bourrée* turn.

BALANCÉ. A movement in three counts. From fifth position right foot front, extend right leg low to the side and *demi-plié* on the right foot, drawing left foot in back of right (knee bent). Step on the ball of left foot; then step on right foot and *demi-plié*. (Left foot is in back of right, knee bent.)

Turns

TOURS CHAINÉS. A series of turns traveling in first position on the balls of the feet or on point.

SOUTENU EN TOURNANT. Turn in fifth position on the balls of the feet or on point. Feet change position while turning, from left foot front to right foot front, and vice versa.

TOURS PIQUÉS. Turn stepping out on one foot (on the ball of the foot or on point) with other foot pointed on the calf traveling in a diagonal or a circle.

PIROUETTE. Turn on one foot (on the ball of the foot or on point) with the other foot pointed and held between the knee and the ankle.

TOUR À LA SECONDE. Turn on one foot (on the ball of the foot or on point) with the other leg extended to the side (ninety degrees).

TOUR EN ATTITUDE. Turn on one foot (on the ball of the foot or on point) with the other leg extended in *attitude*.

FOUETTÉ EN TOURNANT. A series of turns on one foot (on the

ball of the foot or on point) whipping the other leg in a quarter-circle front to side while turning.

TOUR EN L'AIR. From fifth position right foot front *demi-plié,* jump, and turn in the air, changing position of feet. Land in fifth position with left foot front.

Linking Steps

COUPÉ. *Demi-plié* on supporting leg and raise pointed foot with knee bent in front or back of supporting ankle.

PAS DE BOURRÉE. Done on the balls of the feet or on point, keeping feet close together. Step up on left, step up on right, and step down on left into *demi-plié* with right foot pointed in back of ankle (knee bent).

BOURRÉE. Traveling in fifth position on point with knees slightly bent, moving feet rapidly.

GLISSADE. A gliding movement transferring the weight from one foot to the other with the accent on *demi-plié* in fifth position. *Glissade* usually precedes jumps.

FAILLI. From fifth position right foot front *demi-plié,* spring from two feet, and extend left leg *éffacé* back. Land on right foot while the left foot quickly follows passing through first position into fourth position.

Jumps

(All jumps are preceded by demi-plié *and end in* demi-plié.*)*

TEMPS LEVÉ. Jumps from first, second, and fourth positions.

CHANGEMENT DE PIEDS. From fifth position right foot front, jump, changing position of feet in the air, and land in fifth position with left foot front.

133

ÉCHAPPÉ. From fifth position right foot front, jump into second position, then jump into fifth position with left foot front.

ASSEMBLÉ. From fifth position left foot front, slide right foot side and jump from left foot extending right leg side (forty-five degrees). Land bringing both feet together in fifth position right foot front.

JETÉ. A jump transferring weight from one foot onto the other. From fifth position left foot front, slide right foot side, jump from left foot, and land on right foot with left foot pointed in back of right ankle (knee bent).

GRAND JETÉ. A large *jeté* with both legs extended in the air. One leg is extended to the front, the other leg to the back.

GRAND JETÉ EN TOURNANT. A large *jeté* turning in the air landing with one leg extended to the back (ninety degrees).

JETÉ EN TOURNANT. A series of *jetés* with turns traveling in a circle.

SISSONNE FERMÉE. From fifth position right foot front, jump to the left side, extending right leg side (forty-five degrees). Land on left foot with right foot following quickly into fifth position right foot back. Can be done in all directions.

SISSONNE OUVERTE. From fifth position right foot front, jump to the left and raise right foot, pointed below left knee. Land on left foot simultaneously extending right leg to the side (ninety degrees).

SISSONNE TOMBÉE. From fifth position right foot front, jump, descend on left foot, and fall onto the right foot *éffacé* front. Left leg extends *éffacé* back low off the floor.

SOUBRESAUT. From fifth position right foot front, jump *croisé* forward in fifth position with both legs thrust to the back. (Body leans back.) Land in fifth position.

SISSONNE SOUBRESAUT. From fifth position right foot front, jump *éffacé* forward in fifth position with both legs thrust *éffacé* back. (Body leans back.) Land on right foot with left leg extended *éffacé* back.

ROND DE JAMBE SAUTÉ. From fifth position right foot front, jump extending right leg to the side (forty-five degrees) and execute *rond de jambe en l'air* (circle with lower part of leg). Land on left foot with right leg extended to the side (forty-five degrees).

PAS DE CHAT. From fifth position left foot front, raise right leg, bending knee (turned out); jump, raising and bending left knee (turned out) so that both knees are bent in the air. Land on right foot, then left in fifth position left foot front.

PAS DE BASQUE. A combination of movements in three counts involving a slight spring from one foot onto the other with a quarter-circular motion of the leg.

SAUT DE BASQUE. From fifth position right foot front, extend right leg low to the side, transfer weight onto right foot simultaneously turning torso to the right, and jump from right foot, swinging left leg forward and upward. Finish turn in the air and land on left foot with right foot raised and pointed below left knee.

BALLOTTÉ. Jump transferring the weight from one foot to the other repetitively. From fifth position right foot front, jump onto the left foot executing a small *développé* with right leg *éffacé* front, then jump onto the right foot executing a small *développé* with left leg *éffacé* back.

BALLONNÉ. From fifth position right foot front, slide right foot side; jump forward from left foot extending right leg side (forty-five degrees). Land on left foot with right foot pointed in front of ankle (knee bent). Can be done in all directions.

EMBOITÉ. Jump from one foot onto the other, alternating

legs in front of the body with knees bent (turned out).

EMBOÎTÉ EN TOURNANT. A series of half-turns traveling to the right, jumping from one foot to the other alternating legs in front with the knees bent.

CHASSÉ. From fifth position right foot front, jump in fifth position, descend on left, and slide right foot forward, transferring weight to right foot in *demi-plié*. Left leg is drawn toward the right. Repeat jump in fifth position and slide again. Can be done in all directions and is often used as a preparation for *grand jeté en tournant* and *saut de basque*.

Jumps with Beats

(Beats are made with the calves, legs turned out.)

ROYALE. From fifth position right foot front, jump and beat right in front of left and land with right foot in back of left in fifth position.

ENTRECHAT QUATRE. From fifth position right foot front, jump and beat right in back of left and land with right foot in front in fifth position.

ENTRECHAT TROIS. From fifth position right foot front, jump and beat right in front of left and land on left foot with right foot pointed in back of left ankle (knee bent).

ENTRECHAT CINQ. From fifth position left foot front, jump and beat right in front of left and land on left foot with right foot pointed in back of left ankle (knee bent).

ENTRECHAT SIX. From fifth position right foot front, jump and beat right in back of left, beat right in front of left, and land with right foot in back of left in fifth position.

BRISÉ. From fifth position left foot front, slide right foot and extend leg *éffacé* front, jump from left foot drawing left leg toward the right, and beat right in front of left. Land with right foot in back of left in fifth position.

CABRIOLE. A large jump with both legs extended to the front in the air. Swing right leg forward, jump from left foot, and swing left leg upward. (Left is under right.) Beat and land on left foot with right leg extended. Then right foot closes in fifth position. Can also be executed to the back.